The Wonder of Miracles

By the Author

The Power of Resurrection
Anna

THE WONDER OF MIRACLES

BIBLE STORIES THAT LIVE

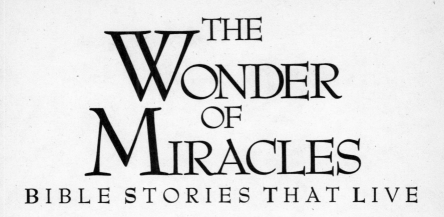

MARGARET A. GRAHAM

1817

Harper & Row, Publishers, San Francisco

Cambridge, Hagerstown, New York, Philadelphia, Washington
London, Mexico City, São Paulo, Singapore, Sydney

FIRST EDITION

Library of Congress Cataloging-in-Publication Data

Graham, Margaret A.
   The wonder of miracles.

   1. Miracles.   2. Bible stories, English.   I. Title.
BS680.M5G68   1988   220.9'505   87-45702
ISBN 0-06-063381-6

88 89 90 91 92   10 9 8 7 6 5 4 3 2 1

For Bubber
who has never known what it is
not to be caring for others

Contents

Preface

There is nothing quite like a good story to vivify an event or to teach truth. The master teacher's Prodigal Son, Rich Man and Lazarus, and other stories are classics in the world of literature nearly two thousand years after their telling. As a long-time teller of stories I have marveled at the Lord's restraint in the stories he told. Never is there an appeal to the emotions, the very heart of any good drama; yet the result is a clarity that leaves the story indelibly impressed on the mind—and, more often than not, on the heart.

In this volume the geographical, historical, and cultural milieu in which the miracles occurred is faithfully given, and restraint was put on an imagination that might easily play up the emotional elements or run afoul of what we know to be true. The primary fictional element is in the thought life attributed to the speaker in each story, but this is done only as a means of letting the reader enter the skin of an eyewitness who asks our questions and gives our answers both verifiable and speculative. There should be no difficulty in drawing the line between essential facts and any flight of fancy that might occur.

With supernatural phenomenon all the rage today, it is imperative that the distinctiveness of the Old and New Testament miracles be understood. Although our's is not unlike other periods in history when "lying wonders" competed with God's genuine miracles for prominence, in this latter half of the twentieth century mysticism threatens to override the ethical tenets of Christianity. Modern mystics think of miracles as something to be had on demand and to be expected as everyday occurrences.

In the history recorded in the Bible, we understand that miracles did not happen every day. Indeed, there were lapses of years, even centuries between epochs of miracles. There were sometimes other supernatural phenomenon (angelic appearances, and so on), and there were remarkable answers to prayer, but the turning of water to blood, the raising of the dead, and the walking on water are the kinds of miracles that occurred during periods of great spiritual darkness for purposes known and unknown to us.

This is not to say that miracles are a thing of the past. Revelation indicates that there will be another great epoch of miracle during the end times. Who knows but what that day is upon us.

One of the distinctive features about a genuine miracle is its ethical nature, for miracles not only reveal the power of God but the character of God. Consider the greatest miracle in the Old Testament, the deliverance of Israel from Egypt. This was achieved through the use of plagues against the Egyptians which, though they brought great blessing to the Israelites, brought great suffering to the Egyptians. What does this tell us about God? Two things: that he is holy, for he judged oppressors of men and idolaters; that he is compassionate, for by discrediting the heathen gods, he sought to win to himself those who were guilty of those offences.

We also learn from a panoramic view of the Bible that miracles effect the plans of the sovereign God as he interacts in time and space. For instance, in the virgin birth we have a miracle of necessity as the Epistles bear out in the Christological passages. Even so, God's miracles are not against nature, but in perfect harmony with his creation. To suspend or countermand a law of nature is within God's prerogative; but often it is in the timing of an event that a miracle is performed, as in the case of the crossing of the Red Sea brought about by a strong east wind.

Miracles sometimes gave credentials to God's servants for authority to act in his name. This was true of Moses, Elijah, and others, but it was not always the criteria. John the Baptist never performed a miracle although he was declared to be God's voice crying in the wilderness. On the other hand, the Lord Jesus Christ would have been highly suspect in his claim to be the Son of God had he not performed miracles.

And what a revelation of Christ comes to us in his miracles. That he would perform his first miracle to prevent the embarrassment of a bridal couple tells us of his tender regard for our smallest concerns. Yet there remains some mystery about his exercise of power; for instance, why he healed some who never asked, and did not heal others.

From among the many miracles recorded in the Bible, the stories selected for this book were chosen to illustrate the epochal and ethical nature of the phenomenon. Although these miracles show the authority of God over nature and the spirit world, there are no stories of the raising of the dead. You will find those accounts in *The Power of Resurrection*. Nor are the miracles recorded in Acts given here, because it seemed fitting that the wonders should culminate in the risen Christ. The continuance of miracles in the Acts of the Holy Spirit since the ascension is a matter of record.

Some of the experiences recorded here are anything but pleasant. As you go down in the belly of the fish with Jonah, may you come up again with a fresh appreciation for what that runaway went through!

Margaret A. Graham
Laurinburg, NC
January 1987

Part I

Old Testament Experiences

Moses

AND THE EGYPTIANS WILL KNOW THAT I AM THE LORD . . .

Scripture Reference: Exodus 3, 5, 7, 11–14

"You should not go to Egypt, young man," my host told me. "We're leaving that country for good. Let me tell you why and what remarkable experiences we've been through in the last nine months."

His brother, Aaron, standing in the tent door, stooped to poke up the fire for a breeze coming across the water bore a chill. The thorns crackled as sparks danced upward in the dusky half-light.

Half-light, because hovering over this vast multitude of a camp was a cloud of fiery brilliance shedding light below. A girl had explained to me that the cloud was leading them. It afforded shade in the daytime and light at night, making it possible for them to travel after sunset. I would have laughed outright but, fearing she was lunatic, I moved on.

I, a goatherd, being young and full of adventure, had left the wasteland of Midian and traveled north for many weeks. Having heard of cities in Egypt that would dazzle the eye, I was determined to see them. Avoiding the main roads, I had strayed across the land bridge above the Red Sea and drifted south along the salt lagoons that bordered the coast. Seeing a multitude of people camping for miles and miles along the shore of Lake Timsah, I ventured to mingle with them to steal what I could and to find out what they were about.

They were a festive crowd, singing and laughing around their fires. Flocks and herds milled about in tidy groups of ten or so; children were squealing, romping everywhere. Among them were some clean-shaven Egyptians, but most of them were not unlike my own people, the men wore beards. Despite their apparent joyousness those who were not Egyptian were marked by a gauntness, the haunted look of a jackal that had long suffered in a trap then been released. There was nothing to recommend these people to an aspiring goatherd.

I moved among them easily, unafraid, and when I grew hungry it was not hard to wheedle from a woman flat bread to eat with my goat's milk. After I had eaten I began to speak of my dreams of seeing Egypt. Impressed with my intelligence and agitated that I was on my way to Migdol, she fetched her brother Aaron, who took me to the tent of their leader, a man named Moses.

Aaron told me that the leader, who was also their brother, was nearly as old as he—and Aaron was in his eighties. I could not believe this man, Moses, was eighty years old for he was well built, strong of voice, and keen of eye. He might have been an imposing figure had he not had a quality about him that I have seldom seen in a man and one I do not admire: he was humble in his manner. Otherwise, why would the leader of such a multitude take notice of a goatherd?

Hearing I was of Midian and had heard of his God, Moses was eager to tell me more.

"In Egypt we have been an oppressed people—not I, but my people, the Israelites." He paused, his shaggy brows knit together in earnestness. "No, I was a privileged youth living as the son of Pharaoh's daughter. I, along with other princes from Syria and Palestine, studied under the most brilliant scribes and wise men in Egypt."

"What did you study?" I asked, eager to hear what might be in store for me if the gods so willed.

"I learned mathematics, astronomy, agriculture, military tactics, art, poetry—many things. It's been so long ago—"

I envied him and wondered how he could leave that life to sit here by the sea in a goat-hair tent.

"I could have continued on in the life of the court," Moses was saying, "but I could not bear the way my people were being treated. I went out to defend one of them and got myself in serious trouble—had to flee the country."

Removing his turban, Moses rubbed the great dome of his head as he reflected. Waiting impatiently for him to tell me more, I happened to see in the shelter of the lean-to a coffin-like box. Seeing my curiosity Aaron whispered in my ear, "The bones of Joseph." I pondered what he said and, stealing a sidelong glance, wondered how I might get a glimpse of the mummy inside, for I had heard something about Egyptian embalming. But the box was sealed as securely as a tomb, and I dare not show myself too inquisitive lest they dismiss me from their company before I knew all I wanted to know about them.

Moses was talking and I turned my attention to him. "I was forty years old when I left Egypt, and I spent the next forty years in the desert of Sinai, in your part of the country, tending sheep. Perhaps you know my father-in-law, Jethro, the priest. Do you know him?"

Aaron excused himself and left.

"I've heard my uncle speak of him," I replied. "My uncle called him Reuel, thinking him a friend of God."

Moses sighed. "Alas, my father-in-law bore with me in my despair. The humiliation of having to flee Egypt was nothing compared to the agony of knowing that all Israelites, except I, were suffering day in and day out. My people, who had once been prosperous shepherds, were made slaves by the Egyptians."

Only inferior people can be made slaves, I thought. *And only inferior people remain slaves. Any slave who proves his worth would be promoted, become a steward or some such. That would not be a bad life.* "What kind of work did they do?"

"They built cities in Goshen to store grain, manned the

irrigation canals, worked in the quarries, made bricks, sweated in the turquoise mines—many an Israelite died in those mines. Many were galley slaves, oarsmen for Egyptian vessels. Some of our women were made harlots. For forty years I roamed the desert of Sinai with my flocks, and never a day passed but what I remembered the agony my family and friends were suffering."

The pain showed yet in his face.

Moses drew in his breath and let it out. "Then one day on Mount Horeb—you should know the place; as bare and steep a mountain as any you see in the Sinai range—high on Horeb I saw a scrubby bush on fire. The blaze concerned me for fear it would spread or frighten the sheep, so I watched it carefully. The bush kept burning, the flames leaping and falling but not dying down. I could not take my eyes off it, wondering how it caught fire and if I should try to put it out. The mountainside, you know, if you have in mind the one I'm speaking of, is almost straight up and down, and I didn't want to climb up there if I didn't have to; but as I watched a gnawing fear grew inside me. Something very strange was going on." His voice quavered a bit. "The bush kept burning and burning but none of it was consumed. Finally I could stand it no longer and, steep as that cliffside is, I began climbing up it. I was within a stone's throw—" The man's eyes widened and, leaning forward, he gripped my arm. So intense was he, his voice fairly rasped. *"God Himself spoke to me!"*

Not waiting to observe my reaction and still holding my arm tightly, he talked excitedly, reliving the experience as vividly as if it was taking place before his eyes. "God told me to go back to Egypt, to go to Pharaoh and request that he let the Israelites leave."

Releasing the grip on my arm, he sat back. A look of remorse was clouding his face. "Afraid to go back to Egypt for fear of what they would do to me, I gave the Lord every objection I could think of. Finally he told me no one still sought my life to avenge my crime, but I had other concerns. You see, I had lived in that court. And all my young life, when I was no older than you, I contended against their gods, their authority, their witchcraft. I knew what I would be up against if I went back." His elbows resting on his knees, Moses rubbed his great head in his two hands. "Yet the Lord God insisted that I return to Egypt and petition Pharaoh to let the Israelites go."

"To let them go? Go where?"

"To a land flowing with milk and honey, the land where the Canaanites live, the promised land."

Canaanites, I thought skeptically. I had heard of those people and that was the last place I would wish to go, but I said nothing. Besides, I could have told him he was headed in the wrong direction if they were going to Canaan, but it was none of my affair.

Moses picked up the rod lying beside him. "Do you see this?" It was not unlike my own rod only longer to fit his height. To spite my uncle, who was very religious, I had carved a falcon head atop mine, but Moses' rod was unadorned.

"More than forty years ago," he said, "I cut this piece of acacia, pruned it, and smoothed it down. For some time it lay in a shed until it was seasoned, then I took it as my rod. Dead for forty years, it is still as sturdy as the day I found it." Gripping it in his strong right hand, he pounded its end against the ground.

It puzzled me that Moses would speak of his rod in the midst of telling me about the great God speaking to him, but I did not interrupt.

Amused by my obvious puzzlement, the leathery skin of his face creased into a smile. "It goes with the story," he explained, and continued. "God told me to throw down this rod and I did." Moses made as if he would throw it on the ground but didn't. "When I threw it on the ground it turned into a snake—a venomous, slithering snake! Believe me, lad, I had seen magicians in Egypt perform tricks with their incantations, but even as a young boy I recognized their lying wonders for what they were: witchcraft."

"Witchcraft?"

"Why, yes. The court teachers used to give us instruction in casting spells and in the tricks of that trade, but I resisted their teaching—wanted no part of it. This changing of my rod was not done by me, not by any incantation, but by God."

He seemed intent that I accept this as truth, and he was not a man one could easily distrust, yet it annoyed me that he did not respect the mystical powers of the priests. Apparently, he believed in an invisible god to the exclusion of all other gods.

"This stick," he said, "became my scepter against all the scepters of Pharaoh—the symbol of God's power. And the snake, it became the challenger of the cobra so revered by Egyptians."

Mention of the cobra reminded me of the camel driver who claimed to have once seen the Pharaoh. Even though I thought the wretch a liar, I listened as he described the headdress of the Great Ruler, the arched neck of a golden cobra curving atop it. At the time I vowed I would find out for myself if what the camel driver said was true.

Moses laid more brambles on the fire and watched as it blazed up. In the firelight his strong features stood in bold relief to the gentle smile that played about his mouth. "In Egypt my brother Aaron and I approached the Israelite leaders first, and they were much impressed by the signs God gave. With their permission we gained an audience with the Pharaoh and requested him to let the Children of Israel go into the desert to sacrifice to our God."

I marveled at the audacity of the man. He talked about an audience with the Pharaoh as if it were a casual event.

"Perhaps you know," he went on to say, "we Israelites make animal sacrifices and that is an abomination to Egyptians; they worship beasts and creeping things."

All life is sacred, I felt, and I quite agreed with the Egyptians in their regard for creatures.

Moses raised his eyebrows mockingly. "The mighty Potentate of all Egypt scoffed at the idea, boasting that he did not know our God and, infuriated, he increased the work load for the slaves."

That, I thought, *is what one would expect of the Ruler of All Egypt.* But my host was undaunted.

"God reaffirmed to me the promise made to Abraham— You've heard of Abraham?"

"Of course. We Midianites are sons of Abraham."

"But not the chosen people," he said, eyeing me for agreement. I did not respond. He went on to explain. "The promises made to Abraham were not given to Keturah's sons but to Sarah's son, Isaac. Isaac passed them on to Jacob, called Israel."

As I suspected earlier on, Moses was indeed a bigot. "What promises?" I asked peevishly.

"Among others, that his descendants would inherit a land, the land of Canaan. God told me that to obtain our release he would use such severe measures Pharaoh would *drive* us out of Egypt.

"The next time my brother and I obtained an audience with Pharaoh, he asked us to show him a miracle. Aaron obliged—threw down his rod and it became a serpent coiling on the ground. I was well aware what would come next. Immediately sorcerers and magicians were summoned, and by their incantations their rods became serpents, too."

The camel driver had told me Egyptian sorcerers had such power, and it excited me to hear that this was true.

A faint smile toyed about the speaker's mouth. "But Aaron's rod swallowed all the other rods and left the magicians speechless."

I felt disappointed but determined not to let it show. Moses' story was not finished. "It was not to be our last contest, my brother and I against the court magicians. In a short time we met again at the river. . . . Ah, the Nile, how beautiful it is at day's end, the sails of ships golden in the sun, the smooth water carrying vessels upriver—cargoes of ivory, spices, gold—"

I couldn't wait to see if a man like Moses could be carried away by the river's beauty. He told me, "It has the sweetest water in the world, the Nile has. That's a blessing because there's no other source of water in Egypt. Spring water is unfit, and wells are seldom found; rainfall is so scarce it can't be collected.

"Do you like wildlife?" he asked, and I nodded. "The riversides teem with wildlife. Men of means hunt along the Nile, bringing down hippos and game birds. As a boy I caught many a fish among the rushes alongside it's banks.

"But I tell you, young man, the Nile can be as capricious as a fractious goat—and," he laughed, "what goat isn't fractious? I've seen the river like an enraged dragon thrashing about, its flood waters drowning stock, sweeping away farms— Despite the dikes, every precaution, there are years when the dragon will not be contained.

"Even so, when the river does not flood that is disastrous too. Without the flooding no silt is left along the banks, and without topsoil there can be no planting." He scooped a handful of the gravelly red earth and let it pour through his fingers. "No farmer can plant this soil."

Moses stirred the embers with a stick and lifted his face toward the sea, breathing in the air. "Having turned their backs on the living God, it's no wonder the Egyptians worship Hapi, the Nile god; their livelihood depends upon that black land along its banks and that smooth water with its south winds sailing their boats upstream. To them the Nile is the 'Father of life,' the 'Father of the gods.' "

For a moment my host was lost in his reverie. I prompted him, eager to hear about the magicians. "You say, sir, that you met the magicians again at the river?"

"Ah, yes. Yes indeed I did. When Pharaoh refused to let the people go, the Lord instructed me to go down to the river where Pharaoh daily performed his ablutions, and announce that God would turn all the water of Egypt to blood. You may know that, due to their worship of animals, blood is an abomination to Egyptians."

That seemed logical to me.

"I did as I was told," Moses said, "and with this rod I struck the water of the Nile. Before our very eyes the water turned crimson, the substance of blood! The priests were horrified. Dead fish floated to the surface, and the fetid stench of the river was nauseating.

"Immediately the magicians Jannes and Jambres stepped forward. And over one of those small stone reservoirs reserved for the poor they rattled their charms, intoned their chants and they too, turned water to blood, for God had sent evil angels among them."

Evil angels indeed, I thought, disbelieving him.

"In no time at all, in all the land of Egypt, not a barrel or pitcher or jug of water was left unpolluted."

The magicians' success gave me little satisfaction—I wanted the wise men of Egypt, by their gods to equal if not best the god of the gloating Israelites. I was careful not to reveal my feelings, and in my most solemn voice I asked, "How did they get water to drink?"

"They dug holes beside the river and as water seeped through the soil, it was purified."

"Oh," I said, and tried to remember a strange story I had heard before—a time when water of the gulf turned red and fish washed up on shore, bloated and dead. A few tides later, if I remembered correctly, the water was clear again. Perhaps the blood of the Nile was nothing more than that, and I shrugged it off.

"Tell me," I asked at length, "was your god ever wont to do such things before—turn sticks into snakes, water into blood?"

"Interesting that you should ask. No, never before in our history did he perform such wonders. On rare occasions he spoke or appeared to our fathers, usually in dreams or visions. And his hand was seen in judgment in the flood and on the Tower of Babel. And, oh yes, in the rain of fire and brimstone on the cities of the plain, but no miracles such as these."

"Why now? Why such miracles now?"

"To deliver his people from slavery. To win the hearts of the Egyptians by exposing their gods for what they are—powerless, false, and abominable to him. Surely you understand how far-reaching the religion of Egypt is. Have you heard of the god Heka?"

"The frog god?"

"Yes." Moses frowned, concerned that I was so familiar with the gods of Egypt. Little did he realize my fascination with all things Egyptian. I wanted to hear more and urged him on. "So, you had trouble with Heka?"

"I was told by God to warn Pharaoh that if he did not let the Israelites leave, hosts of frogs would come up out of the rivers and swamps to plague the land. Pharaoh would not listen, and Aaron stretched the rod over marshes and streams making frogs spring from the waters, leaping everywhere, croaking day and night!"

"Surely the wise men of Egypt could do the same."

"Perhaps," he answered skeptically. "At least they convinced Pharaoh they could. But with frogs already all over everything—in ovens, kneading troughs, and beds—they would be hard put to prove their powers to a thinking man."

The question occurred to me, and I said it before I thought, "Why didn't the magicians send them back where they came from?"

Moses smiled. "They claimed they could bring them up, but they could not make them leave. Pharaoh finally called upon Aaron and me, making a promise he did not keep, asking us to entreat the Lord to get rid of the pests. I asked him at what hour did he want them to leave. Still not convinced that Jannes and Jambres could not take care of the situation, and perhaps thinking the frogs would leave of their own accord, he said,

'Tomorrow.' Agreeing upon the time, I did as he requested.

"The next day, at the very hour he specified, I prayed, and the plague ceased. The miracle showed him plainly that God is in control—that the Lord could dispel the plague at will, something neither Jannes nor Jambres could do; for even if magicians have supernatural power they are not autonomous."

"Autonomous?"

"God is in control of demons and the magicians who serve them."

I changed the subject. "Did Pharaoh let you go then?"

"Oh, no. There were more gods to be dealt with. After the dead frogs were raked into piles and their stench died down, life went on as usual. Israelites, sweltering under the desert sun, were whipped and cursed like animals. Those assigned to the military were worse fed than the horses that pulled the light chariots."

"It is a splendid army, I hear," I said, cautious not to reveal my great admiration. The fame of that military force had reached even me, a goatherd in the desert of Midian. No wonder the army was the pride of all Egypt. I myself would like very much to be a soldier in the service of Pharaoh, and with my brown skin and stiff brown hair I might well pass for a native son once I learned the language, or I might hire on as a mercenary. Their weaponry intrigued me—the curved sword, the rectangular shield curved at the top, their strong horses.

"Are you listening?" he asked, and I assured him I was, when in fact I was not.

"I was saying that after the frogs God told us to bring up gnats, and we were not told to warn Pharaoh as we had done before."

I was not in the mood to hear about a so-called plague which was nothing more than desert people have always endured. I told him, "Swarms of gnats are not unusual in this desert world—gnats and sandflies—all kinds of insects."

"Granted. And that's why the Egyptians worship Seb, Shu,

and the Sacred Beetle, gods and goddesses of the earth, atmosphere, and insects."

That reminded me of the charm the camel driver showed me, the sacred scarab etched on a piece of copper. He told me the beetle was a god, and when I wished to trade for it, poor as he was, he refused to part with it.

"You brought up gnats to prove that your god's power is greater than Seb?" I asked. He nodded. "Then tell me, what did the magicians do?"

"Their conjurations failed. They tried to cast their spell but nothing worked. In fear of losing face, or in astonishment, they avowed that the coming of the gnats was by the power of a god they did not know."

The answer disappointed me. Piqued by the defeat, I thought to show him a thing or two. "Tell me, sir, did your people suffer from the gnats?"

"Yes, they did, but not from the swarms of flies that came next."

"Oh?"

"Ask anyone here or in all the land of Egypt, and they will tell you that Israelites were not bothered by the flies, for in all the land of Goshen where they lived, no flies swarmed."

It was hard to believe, but as much as I hate to admit it, Moses was the kind of man one found hard to distrust. I shrugged my shoulders. "Flies always come swarming in the spring of the year."

"But not with the intensity with which they came this year. You never saw such! They covered everything—an Egyptian dare not open his mouth lest he swallow a mouthful."

"And only you could make them go away?"

"Only *God* could make them go away."

"And he did, precisely when you asked him to?"

"Precisely."

"Then Pharaoh agreed to let you go?"

"No. He offered all kinds of compromises, then reneged. God continued to bring judgments on the Egyptians; but, even

so, not all their gods were affected. They worship so many—
the cat, the cow—" he nodded toward my rod "—and the
falcon, as you know. Were we to sacrifice a lamb or bullock
such as those required by our God, it would have been a
sacrilege to them. They would have slaughtered us. One of
God's severest judgments was against Apis, the bull they worship. He brought a disease on cattle that infected men as well.
The outbreak killed oxen, bulls, cows, calves; men, women,
and children but not the cattle nor people of Israel."

Outside I could hear singing and, raising the flap of the
tent, I saw some people still awake sitting around little fires that
dotted the seashore. In the half-light of the cloud I marveled
again at the hordes of people. How did Moses expect to feed
them? Even though he was familiar with the desert, even if he
knew every source of water to be found, how could he expect
to give that many people water to drink?

Turning back, I wanted to ask him what plans he had for
feeding them; but I first wanted to hear the rest of his story.
"You were saying?" I asked.

"Where was I? Oh, yes. After the disease was taken away,
and still Pharaoh was adamant, God warned us to shelter all
the remaining cattle, beasts of burden and fowls, and to take
cover ourselves lest we be exposed to hail and fire."

I had heard of hail but never seen it. As for the fire, no
doubt he meant lightning.

"In a land where it scarcely ever rains," Moses was saying,
"it was difficult to persuade some people that a hailstorm was
coming. There had never been a dangerous hailstorm in
Egypt. But everyone who regarded the word of the Lord took
protective measures—put their animals under sheds, stayed
indoors themselves, you know. Then God rained down hail-
stones larger than my fist, and balls of lightning ran along the
ground, scorching the earth. Cattle and servants were killed."
He shook his head at the memory. "The flax was destroyed,
fruit trees, grain—no foodstuff was left anywhere in Egypt
except that in the granaries.

"By that time, by the time the hailstorm was in full force, many Egyptians were on our side, believing our God to be the only true God. But not Pharaoh. He feigned repentance, groveled a bit, and promised to let us go, but when the hail stopped falling and the lightning stopped, he resumed his flagrant disregard and flaunted that hateful falcon helmet which he thought protected him. Little did he realize that God was keeping him alive to more clearly demonstrate his power."

I secretly admired the Pharaoh for his obstinancy. The leader of men should be strong as iron. Yet, knowing the end of the story, seeing Moses and his people had escaped, I was well aware that something had made Pharaoh relent, and I wanted to know what it was.

Moses gazed out over the camp, quiet now that the people had settled down to sleep. Returning to his story he again rested his elbows on his knees and, looking at me kindly, spoke softly. "For a day and a night the east wind blew, bringing in locusts that swept in like a blanket between the earth and sky, blotting out the sun. The mere noise of them was terrifying!

"Now, believe me, when I was growing up in Egypt, there were seasons when locusts migrated into Egypt from the south or the west, great hordes of them; but such migrations did not compare with this invasion! You couldn't see the ground for locusts! In minutes whatever had been left from the hail and fire the locusts devoured. Trees were stripped bare, gardens and fields cropped down to the ground! The devastation was so great Pharaoh begged for forgiveness and asked me to pray that God would take away the deadly plague."

Skeptical that so many locusts had come, I felt the proof would be in seeing them swarming somewhere else in the world. I was about to ask him where they went from Egypt, for I had not seen any swarms of locusts in all my travels. As if he read my thoughts, Moses obliged. "Not a locust was left in all the land. A very strong west wind caught them up and carried them into the Red Sea."

Drowned, were they? As good a story as any to explain why the locusts were not roaming the earth, multiplying, devouring every piece of vegetation for generations to come. I was still unconvinced.

Twirling the rod in his hand, Moses' face was grim. "The most terrifying of judgments was then to fall, and it was not to be announced." He laid the rod aside. "It was to befall Ra, the sun-god. I hope you never go to Egypt, but if you do you'll see statues and headresses of Ra, portrayed as a falcon-man with a solar disk over his head. Against such abominable idolatry God brought darkness for three days. The darkness devastated the Egyptians: For if Ra—the sun-god, one of their chief deities—could be overpowered, they had no hope."

"Darkness?" I asked. "You mean the moon walked across the face of the sun?" I had heard old men speak of days when, for a few minutes, the moon blotted out the sun.

Moses shook his head. "No. God sent a hot southwest wind blowing fine dust so thick it shut out the sun. We've seen such dust storms before, cutting a wide swath across the land, but this swift and sudden sand covered Egypt completely, except for the land of Goshen where my people lived. The Israelites went about their work in normal daylight—but over every Egyptian was spread the heavy darkness. No fire nor lamp could be lit in the thick dust—day and night were the same.

"I'm told that in the darkness the Egyptians were terrified by savage beasts prowling about. Can you imagine hearing a snake hissing—rattling its rattlers! They tried their magic arts but couldn't dispel the darkness nor frighten away the animals.

"Oh, the soughing of the wind! We could hear it in Goshen and it was dreadful. They couldn't see so much as a shape before them except for ghastly apparitions, specters that haunted them. The strongest of men, whether ploughman or tradesman, fainted, convulsed in terror. Their children screaming, their women collapsing, they were helpless. For three days they were tormented."

"Your god did that?" I asked, the implication obvious.

"With every right," Moses said defensively. "You must understand the offense idolatry is to the living God."

I did not think of it that way. To me Moses' god was as intolerant as he. "Why didn't your god graciously strike a bargain with the other gods?"

"There is no God but one," he snapped. "Pharaoh offered a compromise, if that's what you mean. In exchange for the restoration of sunlight, Pharaoh offered to allow us to leave on one condition, that our flocks and herds remain behind. This we were unwilling to do."

There, I thought, *the fault lay with this Moses and his god, one as unreasonable as the other.* "What happened then?"

"In a rage Pharaoh drove me from his presence and vowed to kill me if he saw my face again."

Moses stroked his curly beard, his dark eyes somber. "I told Pharaoh that the death angel was to sweep through Egypt killing firstborn sons."

Killing firstborn sons—what kind of a god is that? "Why kill firstborn sons?" I asked, incensed.

His voice rumbling like distant thunder, he bore down on me. "Israel is God's firstborn. It was a fair exchange! And that's not the only reason why. You don't know, do you, that the Pharaoh considers himself to be a god and that his son after him is divine?" He stood up, walked around the fire angrily.

Not until he was composed did he speak again. "For those of us who believed, there was a way to protect our sons. We were told that an innocent lamb could substitute for our firstborn. We were to sacrifice the lamb, sprinkle its blood on our doorposts. 'When I see the blood,' God said, 'I will pass over you.'

"God assured me that before the night was over Pharaoh would drive us out of Egypt. I told Pharaoh, in no uncertain terms, that before this was over all his officials would come to me, bowing down and begging me and my people to leave his country." Moses paced back and forth remembering the scene.

"I was never more angry in my life," he confessed. "Pharaoh's stubbornness and the blind refusal of his subjects to obey God, would cost the lives of thousands.

"We Israelites did as we were told, and some of the Egyptians did likewise and prepared to leave the country with us. Then the death angel came." Moses stopped pacing and sitting down before the fire, his face looked gray and drawn. "It was horrible—all the screaming." He squeezed his eyes shut to block out the memory.

I waited in respectful silence. And then I asked, "How many were killed?"

Moses shook his head. "I have no idea. Every firstborn, from the son of Pharaoh down to the son of the prisoner in the dungeon—even the firstborn of livestock, was stricken suddenly. The wailing, oh, the wailing! There was not a house without someone dead."

I felt my heart racing. How could it be that the divine Pharaoh was humiliated by a man who carried a shepherd's rod not unlike my very own? I could scarcely believe what I was hearing.

From his drawn face I could see the killings distressed Moses more than his victory gave him cheer. He spoke gravely. "During the night Pharaoh, his dead son lying on a stone slab, called my brother and me and told us to leave with all our people and all our possessions. He even asked my blessing.

"We ate our roasted lamb and herbs in a hurry, and the Egyptians urged us to leave quickly, lest they all die. We made our departure in the middle of the night and as we streamed out of Goshen, this pillar of fire appeared above us. The angel of the Lord, it has led us to Pithon, then to Etham, and here to Pi Hahiroth—a fire by night, a cloud by day."

Dawn was showing in the eastern sky. The fire was nearly dead, and as I stared at the white ashes I thought about all I had heard. To say that it dimmed my vision of Egyptian splendor is to put it mildly, but I fought to hold onto my dreams. Truly no such wonders had ever reached my ears before, nor would ever a man hear of anything greater than that Moses, by the power of his god, delivered millions of captive people without unsheathing a sword! I could not deny what my own ears had heard and my own eyes saw, but I was not pleased, for such a feat rendered all my expectations of Egypt to be but vain fantasies.

Then the next day a remarkable turn of events raised my hopes again. An Israelite came tearing down the road from the direction of Baal Sephon. I watched him making his way through the camp, saw him stop and ask a fellow something. The man pointed toward Moses' tent and the Israelite lost no time in reaching us, accompanied by a number of excited people. His face was white as cotton and his whole body shook with fright. "Pharaoh's army is coming!" he announced.

Moses was not perturbed, not in the least surprised!

There followed some discussion among the Israelites concerning the size of the contingent, the direction from which they were coming, and the speed with which they traveled; but from the fear on their faces I knew the Israelites were no match for such an armed force. They discussed the possibility of escape routes but I knew that was out of the question. To the south lay an impassable mountain chain, to the east the sea. To proceed in any other direction would plunge them head first toward their enemy.

Soon the entire camp heard the fateful news and mutinous talk grew stronger with each passing hour. Hurriedly packing up to leave, they knew only that they could not stay there. By sunset we could see the dust rising across the horizon and knew the chariots were rolling toward us. Women started screaming and, gathering up their children, they clasped them to their bosoms.

It was my turn to be ecstatic! At last the Israelites were trapped, and Pharaoh's army would annihilate them—or better, take them back to Egypt as captives.

A big, burly man, his face contorted with anger, shook his fist in Moses' face. "Was it because there were no graves in Egypt that you brought us to the desert to die?" And then he roared, "What have you done to us by bringing us out of Egypt? Didn't we say to you in Egypt, 'Leave us alone; let us serve the Egyptians'? It would have been better for us to serve the Egyptians than to die in the desert!"

The man Moses did not respond in kind but stood calmly waiting until the crowd grew quiet. "Do not be afraid," he said at last. "Stand firm and you will see the deliverance the Lord will bring you today. The Egyptians you see today you will never see again. The Lord will fight for you; you need only to be still."

"Be still?" someone repeated incredulously.

No sooner than he spoke, the cloud that had been above us returned and stood behind the camp. As dusk was followed by darkness, the cloud resumed its fiery brilliance so that the Israelites moved about in light as bright as day.

Hastily taking down their miserable shelters, the people finished packing up their belongings to leave. Aaron yelled to a young man, "Joshua, come help me!" And the two of them proceeded to wrap the coffin in a leather cloth and place it on a two-wheeled cart. "We'll take turns," Aaron said, as Joshua lifted the cart by its handles and pulled it along.

Moses was standing a bit apart from the rest of us, on a gentle slope where many of us could see him, and there he raised his rod over the water of the sea. A sudden east wind began to blow, battering my tunic and making it hard for me to stand against the force. Above the wind I heard excited voices; people pushing forward, clamoring to see. The water was being driven back as easily as if one blew upon broth in a shallow dish! My eyes could scarcely stay open as the wind thrashed about, but I strained to watch as the bottom of the sea appeared in places, the water being scooped up on both sides.

For some time the wind continued blowing steadily, and from the light of the cloud visibility was good. To my astonishment the path being cleared widened rapidly, becoming so wide one could not see where the dry ground ended and the water stood. With my hand I rubbed the falcon head atop my rod and prayed that the army would not stop for the night but come on quickly. It was plain to see, the Israelites could cross the sea!

During the third watch of the night, Moses issued the order to march, ram's horns took up the signal, and the multitude surged forward. Herding their cattle before them, pushing carts, carrying their sick and aged on litters, the people forced their way against the wind.

Thinking I was one of them, they prodded me to move along with them; but I stood my ground, not budging. Pressing my lips against the falcon head, I made a vow praying the chariots would speedily come. *What holds them back?* I wondered anxiously.

Soon I was to know, for when the Israelites were all committed to the path of the sea, the cloud that was light to them became dark behind. I could no longer see the fleeing host for the heavy fog enveloping the land.

Shivering in the dark, I lay down on the ground to escape the battering wind and waited for the chariots to come.

When at last I heard the horses' hoofs and the creaking, groaning chariots, I jumped up and ran to meet them. They were creeping along in the dark gloom, unable to keep their torches burning in the strong wind; their horses snorting, whinneying nervously, afraid in the wind.

I myself could not see and, barely dodging an iron wheel, I realized the danger of being in the way of the lumbering chariots. A charioteer yelled out, "Which way did they go?"

But the roaring wind snatched away my answer and I could not make him hear. Frantically I gestured, showing the way they went, but he had moved past me and I quickly lost sight of him.

I sought higher ground to get out of their way, the slope where Moses had held up the rod. From the sounds of the horses and the cursing, I could tell the men were whipping and forcing the animals forward. No doubt about it, the chariots were rolling down in the path of the sea. I wanted much to warn them, for in the pit of my stomach I knew the path of the sea was dangerous for them, but I could not risk being trampled to death.

My last shred of hope lay in the possibility that Pharaoh's men would overtake the Israelites before the wind stopped blowing, and I sat down to wait, my legs too weak to hold me up any longer.

When the last of the chariots finally rolled past me I felt encouraged. If I calculated correctly the army was rapidly gaining on their prey and, in a little while, would overtake them.

It was then I heard the commotion—wheels grinding, chariots banging into each other—shouted curses and frightened horses neighing! Instinctively, I knew their chariots were bogging down, turning over. Men cried out in panic, "Let's get away from here! The Lord is fighting for them against Egypt."

Noises of confusion increased and, terrified, I got up to run the other way. To keep my balance I leaned against the force of the wind, but I was not halfway down the hill when suddenly the wind stopped blowing, and I fell flat on the ground!

The breath knocked out of me, I lay there trying to regain my wits. The roaring wind had passed me and was sweeping across the desert. In its wake I could hear a thunderous rushing—water swiftly rolling in from both sides! Men screaming!

Horses panic-stricken! I got to my feet and ran back up the slope.

In the time it took me to get up the hill the screaming stopped, and all I could hear above the surging, roaring water was the cawing of a crow.

It was all over. I sank to the ground heartsick.

In the long silence that followed I sat hugging my knees, shaking as if in a chill. As day broke over the horizon the dark cloud had moved beyond, and the sun shone on the calm sea. Below me floated the corpses of men and animals, and in the shallow water near the shore I saw the gilded wheel of one of the Pharaoh's chariots.

I turned my face away, my eyes brimming with tears. Reaching for my rod I looked once more at the carving my hand had made. And then, deliberately, I propped the rod against a stone and with another rock broke it in two. Picking up the falcon head I drew back and hurled it as far as I could. I stood watching it sail end over end in a high arc until it fell into the sea.

2

Joshua

. . . FOR THE LORD YOUR GOD IS GOD IN HEAVEN ABOVE
AND ON THE EARTH BELOW.

Scripture Reference: Exodus 15; Joshua 2–6, 8:30–35

J oshua lay on his back beneath the stars and thought about
the words of Moses he had read that morning. The words
were spoken by God shortly after Joshua and the other eleven
spies had returned to Kadesh-barnea from scouting out the
land of Canaan. The report of walled cities and giants had
frightened the Israelites; and although Joshua and Caleb assured them that the land God had promised them he would
give them, they refused to proceed with the invasion. The
punishment for their disobedience was given by God and
relayed by Moses: "Your children will be shepherds here for
forty years, suffering for your unfaithfulness, until the last of
your bodies lies in the desert. For forty years—one year for
each of the forty days you explored the land—you will suffer
for your sins and know what it is like to have me against you."

Joshua drew a deep breath and let it out slowly. The forty
years were up—forty years of suffering the reproach of the ban
God had laid upon them. *How the Egyptians have mocked us,*
he thought bitterly, *laughed that our God excommunicated us.*
Laughed that the older generations died in the desert, died naturally
or from judgments brought on by more of their disobedience. How
the heathen must gloat that our numbers, in forty years' time, have
not increased.

Joshua thought of Caleb, some years younger than himself,
the only man his age who had been born in Egypt and who

had endured all the experiences in the wilderness. He was yet strong and able in his eighties even as Moses, who died in his one-hundred-and-twentieth year, his physical strength unabated, his eyesight good. It gave Joshua reason to believe that he, too, would maintain his physical vigor despite his age, at least until the work was done.

He missed Moses and again pondered his mysterious death. *Strange that we could not find his grave,* he thought. *I'm sure we went over every foot of Pisgah; didn't find a trace. I wish he were here. I'm not up to the responsibility of leading these complaining people.* He smiled, remembering that Moses had said the same thing.

Joshua rolled over on his side, trying to get comfortable. The intelligence reports told him the walled cities and giants were still in Canaan, even stronger than forty years before, and the only preparation he had been given was, "Cling to the law. Read it, meditate upon it night and day."

Well, he had found it imperative that he do so. There was so much to learn, so much to do, and the promises shored up his faith.

Joshua turned over on his other side, felt under the mat for a pebble that was annoying him. Tossing it aside he thought, *So far, so good,* and relived the victory God had recently given. How formidable the Jordan had seemed until the scouts came back from Jericho. When they came back with the word that the inhabitants were frightened out of their wits because they remembered the "God of the Red Sea," a sudden realization swept through the camp. For years they had been singing the song they sang after the crossing of the Sea; and the prophetic words, "the people of Canaan shall melt away; terror and dread will fall upon them . . ." were apparently being fulfilled. Amazed that the crossing had reached Canaanite ears and that the miracle had been remembered forty years, the Israelites took heart.

As Israel continued waiting on the other side the winding, lazy river rose higher and higher, so that at the ford it was a hundred feet wide and twice the depth of a man. Then the word came from God that the priests were to bear the Ark of the Covenant into the Jordan. As the priests obeyed the water began to go down. Astonished by the water's rapid decrease people babbled excitedly. Theorizing as to what was happening, someone suggested that perhaps the steep banks upriver, their underpinnings washed away by the flood, gave way and slid into the river damming up the water. "That it's happening just now, when we need to cross," a Levite declared, "tells me this is the work of God."

"Could it be that God shook the earth and dislodged the banks?" another asked.

"We would have felt the quake," someone answered.

"I felt a quaking," an old man declared.

As the water lowered the priests waded to the middle of the river and stood there waiting. For hours the water drained from the riverbed into the Dead Sea until finally there was dry riverbed for a distance of twenty miles or more. Given the signal thousands of Israelites, their flocks and herds with them, surged across to the other side.

"As I was with Moses, so I will be with you," God had said; and for Joshua crossing the Jordan confirmed the promise. With twelve stones he had the elders build a cairn in the riverbed and another on the bank to memorialize the crossing. The stones also mocked the circle of stones raised to the planets by heathen worshipers in Gilgal, where Israel was to set up camp.

To Joshua the cairns served as a signal that taking Canaan would be a holy war, as much spiritual combat as military. Remembering the spiritual warfare Moses had waged and won, Joshua did not doubt that God was also equal to the military superiority of giants and walled cities, but he was at a loss to know how the Lord would work.

Israel's weapons—Egyptian daggers and swords, some

hunting knives, axes, and sticks—were no match for the well-equipped Canaanite soldiers with their spears, bows, and swords; their metal and leather armor, helmets, and shields of iron and bronze. Joshua knew only that God was ready to drive out the seven nations inhabiting Canaan, for their iniquity had reached its full measure. For four hundred years God had endured Canaanite wickedness, but he was no longer going to tolerate the gross evils of the inhabitants of the land. Even Egyptians deplored the depravity of Canaanites. No one would deny that the enormity of their decadence deserved the severest of judgment, and God had ordered the extermination of every man, woman, and child so that their atrocious way of life would spread no further nor persist.

After Israel crossed the Jordan they moved ten miles inland and camped at Gilgal. There Joshua had the people pen up their lambs in anticipation of the observance of the Passover; but before the feast all males would be circumcised to acknowledge their covenant relationship with God, and to signify the end of God's ban. As hands wielded the sharp knives Joshua declared that with the rite of circumcision they were rolling away the reproach of Egypt. No longer could an Egyptian taunt Israel saying their God had forsaken them, for now God had opened the Jordan as he had opened the Red Sea. Israel's punishment was over! It was a momentous relief; so much so, Joshua instructed his family that when he died the knives used for circumcision were to be buried with him in his tomb.

After the Passover Joshua did not sleep well, and from time to time he lay gazing up at the night sky wide awake. Ever since he left Egypt he had slept with the fiery cloud overhead. Now it was gone even as the manna was gone; he would have to get used to bread made from beaten grain. For so long they had taken the cloud and the manna for granted . . .

After a while Joshua got up, lit a lamp, and brought out the maps the spies had made of the desert and of Canaan. He spread them on the ground and studied them carefully. With his finger he traced the route they had taken after leaving Kadesh. Again he was satisfied that the journey around Edom was not without purpose. Coming by that route they avoided the fortifications in the south of Canaan, and the forty-year delay of the invasion had allowed time for Egyptian oppression to weaken Canaan while at the same time outlasting Egypt's military interests in Canaan. When Israel had finally engaged the enemy on the other side of Jordan, Moses' victory over the Amorites under Sihon and Og dealt a blow to Canaanite morale that made them feel far less invincible.

Still, Joshua pondered, *I don't know how we will take Jericho.* The city was an oasis edged by a barren waste of chalk. As he pored over the map of Canaan, he reviewed Jericho's strategic position—a fortress set upon high ground above the ford of the river—guarding the trade route from the east. On the west bank of the river the route broke into three branches, one going south to Hebron, another to Jerusalem, and the third to the north towards Bethel and Shechem. There was no other entrance to the midsection of Canaan other than this one protected by the double-walled fortress. Joshua shook his head. *Conquering Jericho is humanly impossible,* he said to himself.

As daybreak lightened the eastern sky Joshua snuffed out the lamp, rolled up the maps, and decided to go up and reconnoiter the city. From Gilgal Jericho was a good two miles over rough terrain. His wife came out of their tent, sleepy-eyed and looking worried. "Did you sleep?"

He shook his head. "Go back to bed. It's early."

By the time the sun rose above the Jordan plain Joshua had climbed to a promontory jutting out over the valley. From the overlook he gazed toward the forest of balsam and palm trees that lay to the southwest. The lofty battlements of Jericho were on the other side of the trees, and back of the fortress were steep limestone cliffs. The scene reminded him of the palm forest of Memphis, close by the pyramids.

A gentle breeze swept past him, stirring the dry brush. From his position Joshua could look down on the double walls encircling the city. The inner wall surrounded the ridge of the hill, the outer wall ran along the base of it. He estimated the inner wall to be ten to twelve feet thick, the outer wall half as thick. Made of sun-dried brick, the two walls were twenty-five to thirty feet high and were separated by a space six feet wide. Houses and shops were inside the enclosure; and on the walls, built on timbers spanning them, were flat-roofed houses.

The snapping of a branch startled him . . . then another. Carefully Joshua turned, and there—standing less than twenty feet away—was a soldier, sword drawn. Hesitating, Joshua eyed the man, not knowing what to do or say; then cautiously he asked, "Are you for us or for our enemies?"

"Neither," he answered, "but as commander of the army of the Lord I have now come."

Joshua gasped then fell on his face, worshiping. In a barely audible whisper, he asked, "What message does my Lord have for his servant?"

The Commander replied, "Take off your sandals, for the place you are standing is holy."

His hands trembling, Joshua untied the thongs that bound his sandals, loosed them, and laid them aside.

The Commander then told him that Jericho, its king and its militia, would be given over to him. Joshua listened, his head bowed, as he was given instructions for the battle.

For the next six days they were to march around Jericho once a day and, on the seventh day, seven times; the men of war heading the line of march, followed by seven priests preceding the Ark of the Covenant and blowing ram's horns; the people bringing up the rear. They were not to make any noise as they marched, raise no battle cry; but on the last trip around, when they heard the long blast of ram's horn, they were to shout. "Then the wall of the city will collapse and the people will go up, every man straight in."

As soon as all the instructions were given Joshua sensed

that the Commander had departed, yet out of reverence he
waited. Finally he raised his eyes. No one was anywhere near,
nor was there evidence of anyone having been there. Only the
scent of cedar was in the air.

Joshua ran his tongue over his dry lips, waited a moment
for his senses to recover, then made his way back to the en-
campment. That morning he gathered the officers together,
instructed them in all the Lord had told him, and they in turn
spread the word.

"The city and all that is in it are to be devoted to the Lord,"
Joshua told them. "Only Rahab the prostitute and all who are
with her in her house shall be spared, because she hid the spies
we sent."

The silver and gold and all vessels of brass and iron were
to be given to the treasury of the Lord; everything else was to
be burned and destroyed.

The next morning, as the people of Israel assembled for the
task ahead of them, the men of war took up their positions at
the head of the march. Priests—their linen robes resplendent
in the sun, trumpets held in readiness to herald the approach
of the Ark of the Covenant—fell in behind the army. The Ark,
borne on the shoulders of four priests, was covered from view;
and behind the Ark nervous, excited Israelites crowded along
the slopes. Joshua gave the signal to march, and the stream of
Israelites straggled up the steep approaches to Jericho.

After the laborious climb officers herded the stragglers into
an orderly line of march, without gaps or irregularities. Caleb
stood by Joshua's side watching, both men observing the non-
descript men of war, the fledgling Israeli army. "Remember,
Caleb, the rag-tag army we had at Rephidim when we drove
off the Amalekites?"

Caleb smiled. "We could never have won the battle had it
not been for God. But for the raised rod we would have gone
down in defeat." He rubbed his forehead. "When I think of

Aaron and Hur holding up Moses' arms I think of us, Joshua. The difference is that we're without a rod, you know."

"Aye. But not without God."

The trumpets were blasting away, raising a jubilant herald going in and out around the eastern wall. "I can imagine the frenzy going on inside Jericho right now, can't you, Caleb? Sentinels in the towers relaying the approach of our people— officers shouting frantic orders— 'Double-man the east gate!' Imagine their perplexity when our people march past the east gate without attacking."

"And the south gate, and the west gate, and the north gate. It's a war of nerves," Caleb said.

"The trumpeters have rounded the corner now, I can barely hear the sounds of them. The strange silence of our people must be unnerving to the enemy."

"They're bound to have the jitters, Joshua."

On into the morning they watched the procession. By the time the last of the Israelites were beginning the march around Jericho, the first marchers were rounding the last corner. "See," Caleb said, pointing, "they've completely surrounded the city!"

"I wonder what the enemy is thinking now."

"That we'll attack, no doubt."

"And when we don't—?"

"That we've examined the situation and decided not to attack."

"Yes, I guess they'll congratulate themselves—think we're retreating." Joshua smiled. "But we'll be back tomorrow."

Around campfires that night spirits were high. Women sang to the accompaniment of tambourines, children danced. Men were sharpening blades and talking. One of Joshua's sons asked, "Did you see the scarlet rope?"

"What scarlet rope?" his wife responded.

"Dangling over the wall from Rahab's house."

"I didn't see any rope. Where was it?"

"On the corner. Like other houses, her house is built on timbers laid across the walls."

"Show it to me tomorrow."

"I will if you're alongside me. Rahab's family is the one we're supposed to spare."

"I know."

And so the marching continued for six days, and in that time every Israelite had identified Rahab's house. On the seventh day, on the seventh trip around Jericho, a long blast on a trumpet set the people shouting. Suddenly a wave of motion ran the length of one swaying wall: jagged cracks and fissures split the walls top to bottom—bricks toppling—segments of the walls collapsing, falling flat, jarring the earth! The outer wall was falling outward, stones and bricks crashing down the hillside—a deafening roar of rumbling earth—the inner wall falling inward, burying homes and shops, dust quickly billowing upward!

Like an army of ants Israel's men of war clambered over the piles of stones, wielding weapons. Most of the enemies lay buried beneath the rubble, and survivors were too panic-stricken to resist. An officer sat dazed on the ground as Joshua ran him through, and a male prostitute laughed hysterically. Animals ran amuck—sheep bleating, camels braying. The dead lay in pools of blood—the injured strewn about, screaming, moaning—lying still. Fires blazed, flames crackling, black smoke billowing into the air. Joshua's men made haste searching for the metals they were to spare.

The battle was a bloody, gory task. When every human voice was stilled, Joshua obeyed the Lord's command and ordered the torch be set to whatever remained. The fire spread quickly, the wind sweeping the flames higher and higher, the heat of it unbearable. Joshua ordered the men to withdraw.

Drenched with sweat and blackened from the smoke, Joshua made his way to the shelter of the palms. A soldier scooped water from one of the fountains and handed him the cruse. Joshua gulped down the cold water then dipping the cruse again he poured water on his head, then over his hands to wash away the blood. Handing his dagger to an aide to clean, Joshua asked him to find him clean clothes while he stripped off the bloody garments and bathed himself. The aide returned with a robe and, handing it to Joshua, he stooped down to wash the blood from the dagger's handle and blade. "I'll have this sharpened for you, sir," he said, and taking the dirty clothes he left.

Joshua dressed then sank to the ground, too weary to talk. Fires roaring in the rubble of Jericho sent flames leaping up against the night sky, the smoke boiling upward. Joshua closed his eyes and tried to shut out the horrors he had seen.

The last of the troops had come down the hillside lugging weapons and tools of iron they had found, and sacks of gold and silver to be used in the service of God. Depositing the treasure in a pile, they joined others at the fountains as Joshua listened to their excited talk. "The earth shook, I felt it," one of them said.

"You only felt the jarring when the walls fell," another argued.

"It was more than rumbling."

"I know. I felt it too!" a third one insisted.

"Whatever," the first one said, "it was the hand of God."

"I agree. If the walls had fallen the other way, we'd have lost the battle."

The night wind rattled the dry palm fronds overhead, and Joshua longed for sleep; but sleep was out of the question. The fire lighting up the night sky, struck by downdrafts of wind, bore the smoke in upon them. His eyes smarting, Joshua fanned his face and waited for the day.

Before morning a heavy rain began to fall, and by the time daylight came the flames had died down. Smoke still rose from the rubble and drifted over the valley like an avenging spirit, its wet, burnt smell hanging heavy in the air. Overhead, vultures were circling lower and lower over the debris.

Many of the men were climbing back up to survey the ruins. Joshua ate a few dates and curds of milk, then climbed the hill to join them. Covering his nose and mouth with his sleeve because of the smell, he saw that fires were still burning and timbers smoldering. Only one corner of the walls remained intact, the sides and roof of a house supported by the walls were still standing; he thought this might be Rahab's house. A vulture perched atop it, the bird's naked neck craned to survey the feast below.

Burned and blackened bodies lay in great heaps, trapped by collapsed roofs and debris. Blackened stones, charred wood, white ashes were everywhere. Beside Joshua's foot an arm protruded from a pile of bricks, the hand clutching a doll-like thing. Joshua reached down, pried open the fingers to release the small statue. Examining the crude female figure carved from clay, he saw that it was the fertility goddess, Asherah. Striking the idol against a brick, he broke it in pieces. Stooping down, he gathered up the pieces and one by one crumbled them in his hands.

In the days that followed the Israelites suffered a setback when they attacked the outpost of Ai. In the debacle thirty-six of their men were killed as they retreated. Grief-stricken Israel was furious! Joshua flung himself prostrate before the Lord. Where is God and all his promises? This miracle-working God—where is he?

God told Joshua to get up and take stock, and in so doing he was given the reason for the disaster. The defeat was due to the sin of Achan who had broken the ban on Jericho by stealing gold, silver, and a Babylonian robe from the plunder. When the offender was punished Joshua was able to lead the army in an ambush strategy that enabled them to take the outpost.

During the brief respite that followed the battle, Joshua led Israel to Mt. Ebal twenty miles north of Ai. With Jericho demolished and neighboring towns subdued, the route north was theirs. The mountain and its sister, Mt. Gerizim, were close by Shechem where Abraham built the first altar in the Promised Land, the first place he pitched his tent, and the place where God spoke his earliest promises. This was the place where Jacob had bought a parcel of ground and dug a well; the portion he bequeathed to Joseph and the place where Joshua would bury Joseph's bones.

Joshua's eyes brimmed with tears as he stood on that historic ground. Today Israel would climax everything that had gone before and he, Joshua, was the man privileged to lead the witness.

Finally all Israel was assembled to worship God and pledge themselves to the keeping of the law. As Joshua surveyed the scene before him he was overcome with the significance of what he was about to do. A sea of people stretched as far as the eye could see, their tribal banners waving in the morning breeze. Half of the tribes stood on Mt. Ebal, half on Mt. Gerizim, a narrow valley separating them. The formation made a natural amphitheater. Joshua stood with the priests and Levites in the valley, the Ark of the Covenant in the center, the scrolls before him. On plastered stones Joshua had written all the words of the covenant. Now the time had come to read aloud the curses and the blessings.

Breathing in the aroma of sacrifices drifting on the air

Joshua unwound the scroll, lifted his voice, and began reading aloud the words of the law. The words carried easily to the farthest listener and echoed back to him. First the blessings of the law were read, and the Israelites standing on Gerizim shouted, "Amen!" The sound reverberated between the hills. The heavy scroll trembled in his hands as Joshua read the curses for disobeying the law. Those on Mt. Ebal shouted a resounding, "Amen!"

For some time no one moved, an attitude of profound reverence pervading. Finally Joshua began to rewind the scroll. His wife, his sons, and their families rejoined him as the multitude dispersed.

One of the priests asked, "When are we going to set up the tabernacle?"

"Soon. When we've rid the region of enemies."

"Where?"

"At Shiloh, halfway between Shechem and Bethel. Our father Jacob bought a tract of land there and dug a well. That's where we'll bury Joseph's remains."

3

Elisha

NOW I KNOW THERE IS NO GOD IN ALL THE WORLD EX-
CEPT IN ISRAEL.

Scripture Reference: 2 Kings 2–4:7, 38–44; 5–6:23

Elisha received what he had asked for, a double portion of
Elijah's spirit—or, as the patriarchs would have stated it,
the spiritual birthright, the double portion of the firstborn to
become the leadership successor. And this fact was confirmed
at the Jordan when Elisha used the mantle, the symbol of his
authority, to part the water of the river.

As he came out of the river on the Jericho side Elisha could
not ignore the sensation that exhilarated him. Realizing that
Elijah's last miracle was his first, he was assured that God had
passed the responsibilities and enablements of Elijah to him.
The realization made him think of Joshua's appointment when
God told him, "As I was with Moses so I will be with you."
He was confident that as God was with Elijah, so he would be
with him.

Well aware of the fifty sons of the prophets watching him,
Elisha strode toward them with the confidence only God can
give. A little older than most of them, and younger than some
of them, Elisha knew he would be put to the test. He stopped
for a drink of water at a fountain in the palms and waited as
they approached him.

The prophets were hesitant—one of them nudged another,
prompting him to speak. The spokesman, unsure of Elisha's
new position among them, faltered in his speech; but essen-
tially expressed the doubt that Elijah was truly transported,

believing rather that the whirlwind had scooped him up and dropped him somewhere. Their consensus understood, all the prophets began talking at once, loudly and insistently. A search must be made for their beloved mentor, and no time must be lost lest Elijah be lying injured some place.

At first Elisha refused them permission, knowing their mission would be futile; but when they persisted he allowed them to go. Eagerly they forded the river and spread out on the other side to comb the Mount of Olives and its environs.

As for Elisha, he remained in Jericho. After three days of painstaking searching in every ravine, every thicket, every possible place Elijah's body might have fallen, the men came back to the city satisfied that Elijah had indeed been translated to heaven.

Convinced of the truth, the sons of the prophets transferred their respect for Elijah to Elisha. Their wives brought supper to the compound where the single men lived, and as they were eating some men of the city gathered in the courtyard to visit, excited over the result of the search. An old scribe was holding forth on the historic significance of the event. "Not since Enoch has any such thing happened in the history of mankind!"

A young tanner, standing apart from the others, was half hidden by the shadow of a wall.

"Elijah's ascension will forever be one of the wonders of the world!" someone exclaimed.

"To think that it happened in my lifetime—" the scribe marveled. "And close by where we live! To think: right here, near Jericho! Jericho, the cursed city."

The inquisitive tanner could no longer keep quiet. "Cursed?"

The old man sniffed in annoyance that the tanner was so bold. A dealer in animal skins was abhorrent, not only because he worked with unclean animals but because the processes by which he tanned the hides left him with an odor that was very offensive. "Surely you know Jericho was cursed when Joshua's people brought down the walls. Anyone who would rebuild its walls would pay dearly." The scribe turned his face away and reviewed the matter for the other listeners. "Anyone who would try to rebuild the walls would lose all his sons. In the beginning he would lose his firstborn, and by the time he set up the gate his last child would die."

"Did that ever happen to anyone?" the tanner persisted.

"To Hiel," he said and spat, "cursed be his name."

A youth among the sons of the prophets asked, "Sir, do you think the curse has anything to do with our bad water? Here we are in a beautiful situation, the town unwalled, these towering palms unlike any trees in all Judah or Israel, but some of our springs have gone bad and our wives are barren. Is this because of the curse?"

Elisha had finished his meal and was standing in the court-yard yawning and stretching himself. The scribe, looking his way, referred the question to him. Elisha raised his eyebrows quizzically and, characteristically, the student prophets all began talking at once, explaining the problem. They thought the bad water made their wives miscarry, ruined their crops. Without answering their questions Elisha moved toward the fountains that supplied the town, the entire retinue following.

When they reached the limestone grotto where the water flowed clear and cold from an underground spring, one of the prophets scooped up a handful and held it close to Elisha's nose. The noxious odor was faint but definitely present. "The water is bad and the land is unfruitful," the man repeated.

Elisha shook his head wearily and thought, *If only people were as much concerned about the purity of their lives as about the purity of their water, Judah would not be in the position it was in.* Jehoshaphat, king of Judah, was determined to bring about reconciliation with the northern kingdom, Israel; and disregarding Baalism, the offensive state religion of Israel, he had leaned over backward to placate King Ahab and his wife Jezebel. As conciliatory measures Jehoshaphat named one of his sons, Jehoram, after the son of Ahab and gave that son in marriage to their daughter—all to effect an alliance with Israel.

But Elisha could forsee the evil that would come to Judah through that unholy union. Jehoshaphat's good intention would miscarry and wreak havoc on Judah.

"Bring me a new bowl," Elisha asked, "and put salt in it." The cruse they brought him was a flat metal dish; and as they poured in the salt he knew they were well aware of its potency. The salts and minerals of the Dead Sea killed freshwater fish brought down by the Jordan; and salt was the disenfectant with which they bathed their newborn infants, the preservative they used to cure meats and fish and to pickle olives, and the most common seasoning for their food. By salt covenants were sealed, sacrifices were made, and fertile land was cursed.

Elisha, holding the bowl just above the spring, threw the salt into the pool. "This is what the Lord says: 'I have healed this water. Never again will it cause death or make the land unproductive.'"

The sons of the prophets hesitated to taste the water; but the young tanner reached for a gourd, dipped it in the spring, and brought it to his mouth. Before he drank his dark eyes peered over the gourd, roving over the assembled crowd contemptuously. Taking a sip he began to smile, and then he drank until he drained the gourd.

A burst of applause was given him. "Bring the vessels! Bring the vessels!" they cried. Soon everyone was busy drawing water.

During the excitement Elisha slipped away from them and headed toward Bethel. There was barely time to reach the city before nightfall, and Elisha knew the Bethel colony of prophets would be waiting for him to tell them the details of Elijah's translation. As he hurried along he was thinking of how recently he had come down this road with Elijah by his side. In his heart Elisha felt sorrow that he would never again serve the man who had been a spiritual father to him, and he felt keenly the responsibilities that now were his as the spiritual father of the servants of God.

As Elisha hiked up the road he thought about the anxiety of the sons of the prophets in Bethel as they had stood about that day, bewildered by what was about to come to pass, knowing Elijah was going to be taken from them. *By now they've heard of Elijah's translation,* he told himself, *and they'll be full of questions. I wonder what effect the news has had on Baal worshipers?*

Bethel was not only the home of God's prophets, it was once the site of a state shrine raised to one of Jeroboam's calves. The hideous wooden image, covered with plates of molten gold, had at a later time been supplanted by Jezebel's images of Baal; but now the calf was again the preferred idol. Elisha wondered if anyone in Bethel remembered the curse laid upon the calf idols and priests of Bethel. Israel's new king, Jehoram, in defiance of his mother, Jezebel, was reestablishing calf worship as the state religion.

Elisha felt the irony of the situation. *It doesn't make much difference,* he thought, *whether they worship the calf or Baal.* Religious opposition in Bethel was keen, and Elisha knew he must confront the opposition with courage and the power of God.

Breathing hard as he climbed the incline of the *wadi,* Elisha lamented the abject depravity of Bethel. Early on Abraham had worshiped God near Bethel. And Jacob gave the place its name after receiving a vision there. It seemed incredible that a town could sink to idolatrous degradation after enjoying such a unique heritage of God's favor. But his thoughts were interrupted by the sound of running footsteps on the road in back of him, and he turned to see who it was. Even at a distance he recognized the tanner, a youngish man. As he drew closer Elisha noticed how thin and soft his beard was.

The tanner hailed him. "Sir, my name is Gehazi." Speaking all in a rush, the words tumbled out as if memorized. "For six months I have been studying the scrolls borrowed from one of the servants of God in Jericho. I have not kith nor kin dependent upon me. I am able bodied, as you can see, and I am eager to serve."

"Well, young man, what is it you want?"

Gehazi leaned forward in a humble bow. "If I could but serve you, sir. Wash your feet, see that you have a mount to ride, a place to sleep."

"What about your trade?"

"I've given it up, sir, as of a week ago. It is hardly the trade of a religious man. I want to better myself, seek a higher calling; and hearing your master was taken from you, I knew I must move quickly lest another be chosen ahead of me."

"Very well," Elisha replied, without giving the matter much thought. Nervously, Gehazi fell in step behind him, following at a respectful distance. "I'm going to Bethel," Elisha told him.

"Ah, yes, Bethel, formerly called Luz." Gehazi cleared his throat and continued in a high-toned, authoritative manner as if reciting a lesson learned. "Bethel, 'the house of God,' so named by our father Jacob after his vision of angels and the ladder, and hearing the voice of God."

"The 'gate of heaven,' " Elisha added.

"I was about to say that, sir." Emboldened, the tanner drew alongside, eager to engage the heir apparent in conversation, careful to agree quickly with every word the prophet said and anxious to add some knowledgable comment of his own. His obsequious behavior annoyed Elisha, and he regretted that he had so quickly agreed to take him on.

"The underground passageway at Bethel was the clever means our father David used—"

Elisha did not care to hear his prattle, and thinking upon his own summons to serve Elijah he recalled that it had been initiated by God himself. *But,* he thought, *mine was a case of a different kind. The mantle Elijah put about my shoulders portended my eventual succession to leadership. Gehazi's servitude has nothing to do with succession. Surely the tanner has no such ambition.* But Elisha could not deny what he had already detected in the man, the two vices of opportunism and greed of place.

The climb to Bethel was steady, and Elisha did not take time to rest. Gehazi rattled on, "In Bethel unbelief is rampant, sir. Despite the king's outlawing of Baal worship, it is still practiced, much to the delight of Jezebel. The sons of the prophets there suffer much abuse from their wicked neighbors. You should hear the way they are maligned—but need I tell you?"

Elisha did not like to talk about the sacrilegious people of Bethel, for sooner or later God would judge them. Furthermore, he did not wish to be guilty of their sin of gossip. The town was rife with malicious false accusations. Rubbing his bald head he thought about the rumor they spread in Bethel about him. Because he was bald and lepers also lost their hair, evil tongues circulated the lie that Elisha had leprosy, a disease that made him unfit to mingle with healthy people.

The highlands of Ephraim were cooler than the Jordan Valley from where they had come; and, reaching the last lap of the way, they welcomed the relief. Climbing up the side of the *wadi*, they came to a hillock that afforded a wide view of the ravine they had traveled. As they stood there catching their breath and surveying the valley, Gehazi pointed to a movement in the brush far below. They followed the movement until a bear broke through into a clearing. Watching as the light-colored bear loped down the *wadi* in search of prey, Gehazi remarked, "I pity the lamb that crosses his path,"

"Or the goat or hare."

"I've seen those Syrian bears splashing upriver, catching fish."

"Have you heard them clawing trees in the wood?"

"To sharpen their claws?"

"To get at honey, I'd say." Elisha smiled. "I wouldn't risk getting near enough to find out."

"Nor I, sir. I once knew a shepherd who had a lot of trouble with bears killing his sheep. He decided to set traps for them and one day he caught a cub in one of the traps." Gehazi shook his head soberly. "The shepherd scarcely lived to tell about it.

You should have seen what that mother bear did to him! Left him a cripple for life."

The bear out of sight, they turned to continue on to Bethel. The town was situated on a low-lying hill surrounded by two deep *wadis,* and as they rounded a bend Bethel came into view. Up ahead they could hear voices and, pausing to listen, they saw a gang of youths coming toward them brandishing clubs. "Uh-oh," Gehazi said. "Looks like trouble."

Seeing the prophet, the youths ran toward him taunting, "Go on up, you bald head; go on up you bald head."

Elisha realized they'd heard of Elijah's going up to heaven and were challenging him to do the same.

As the young men surrounded him they pushed and shoved him from side to side, knocking his staff from his hand. One of them thrust a miniature of Baal in Elisha's face, a soldier figure with helmet and skirt, a club in his right hand, a spear in his left. Mocking and jeering, the unruly youths snake-danced past him and went chanting on their way. "Go on up, you bald head! Go on up!"

Elisha shouted after them, "I curse you in the name of the Lord!" to which they only laughed the louder, flinging stones and insults back at him.

When they were out of sight, Elisha picked up his staff, smoothed his rumpled clothes. "Are you all right?" he asked Gehazi.

"I'm quite all right, sir," and the two of them continued on their way. "Perhaps they were drinking," Gehazi suggested.

"Drinking or not, they profane the Name when they make mockery of what God has done."

No sooner had he spoken than blood-curdling screams split the air! They turned around and saw boys running in every direction, clothes torn off, blood streaming. Enraged bears chased after them, easily overtaking them, and mauled them right and left. Elisha watched helplessly as a bear no more than twenty feet away reared up on her hind legs, towering over a cowering youth. With one swipe she knocked the boy into the air. Losing sight of him, she dropped on all fours and went growling after another youth.

Elisha hurried to the young man's aid. Turning him over he saw the bloody flesh ripped from shoulder to thigh, but the victim was still alive. Using his outer robe Elisha did what he could to stop the flow of blood but he had no means of treating all the wounds.

Sounds of the rampage were growing distant, for the bears were crashing through the brush going down into the ravine. In their wake they left mutilated bodies strewn about. Sounds of moaning and incoherent babbling came from every direction . . .

"Gehazi, go into the city. Tell the sons of the prophets to bring me medicine, litters, and splints."

Quickly, Gehazi turned to obey. Elisha called after him, "Have someone tell the parents."

As he waited Elisha went from one youth to another, checking pulses, wounds, and broken bones. He counted forty-two boys, all maimed, blinded, or crippled, but none were dead. *What a terrible judgment,* he thought. *What needless suffering! This didn't have to be; they brought it on themselves. As long as they live they'll bear the marks of their sin.*

In the weeks that followed Elisha and his servant went up to Mt. Carmel and backtracked to Samaria, the capital of Israel. As they walked the streets of Samaria, Elisha showed Gehazi the magnificent ivory palace of Ahab and pointed out the Phoenecian influence in its architecture and art forms.

Gehazi remarked, "I understand Jezebel does not live here but in Jezreel."

"True."

"Thanks to Elijah, Jezebel's influence is on the wane,"

Gehazi said. "Even her son Ahaziah shunned Baal, sought the gods of Ekron. And now his brother, Jehoram, has removed the Baal from Samaria and favors calf worship." With a pompous wave of his hand, he added, "Is not that an improvement?"

Elisha frowned. "You think like Jehoshaphat. He thinks his compromises have lessened the antagonism toward the Lord, but the swing away from Baalism is not toward the Lord but to other gods."

"But can you blame Jehoshaphat for trying?" Gehazi argued.

"I learned when I plowed my father's farm that an unequal yoke never works. An ox and an ass can't plow together, and neither can a righteous man be partner with a heathen. Jehoshaphat should have learned that when he went into that trading venture with Ahaziah. They built a fleet of cargo ships at Ezion Geber and planned to be partners in trade, but the ships never sailed; they sank in the harbor."

A group of officers was coming out of the palace, their expressions grave and their conversation somber. Gehazi observed them carefully. "Jehoram has taken a count of military age men. Something serious is astir. It sounds as if he has sent for Jehoshaphat. If you ask me, I think it means war."

"War?"

"Do you think Jehoram is going to stand for Moab's rebellion as his brother, Ahaziah, did?"

"No, I don't think he will," Elisha replied. "He needs that 'mutton king's' tribute."

"I understand King Mesha had been sending Israel a hundred thousand lambs and a hundred thousand rams with their wool every year."

"That's correct; and without it Israel's revenue is considerably reduced," Elisha said. "Jehoram has sent for Jehoshaphat because Jehoshaphat defeated a coalition of forces from the other side of Jordan, Moab, and Ammon. The victory was not in Jehoshaphat nor his army. Judah went into battle praising

God, and when they reached the battlefield they found nothing but dead bodies. Their victory was a miracle."

"If Israel marches against Moab, will you go with the troops?"

"It's customary. Baal prophets accompany the fighting forces. Why shouldn't I?"

In a few days Elisha and Gehazi were following the armies of Israel and Judah around the southern end of the Dead Sea on their way to engage the fighting men of Moab. This route was longer than if they had crossed the Jordan north of the Sea, but it led them into Edomite territory where Israel and Judah enlisted the support of that ally.

In the treacherous heat of the salt flats, the troops ran out of water. Searching everywhere, they found none; and Jehoram, king of Israel, swore, "What! Has the Lord called us three kings together only to hand us over to Moab?"

Jehoshaphat spoke gently in order not to offend. "Is there no prophet of the Lord here, that we may inquire of the Lord through him?"

An officer was quick to answer. "Elisha, the son of Shaphat, is here. He used to pour water on the hands of Elijah."

Jehoshaphat was delighted. "The word of the Lord is with him."

Gehazi led the three kings to Elisha's tent. The prophet's face was stormy as he glared at Jehoram. "What do we have to do with each other?" he snapped. "Go to the prophets of your father, and the prophets of your mother."

Jehoram answered quickly. "No, because it was the Lord who called us three kings together to hand us over to Moab."

Elisha regarded him with disgust. "As surely as the Lord Almighty lives, whom I serve, if I did not have respect for the presence of Jehoshaphat, King of Judah, I would not look at you or even notice you." He turned to Gehazi. "But now bring me a harpist."

Quickly a musician was summoned. As the soldier strummed the chords, the words of David's psalms came to Elisha's mind, calming him and settling his concentration.

After a while God spoke to Elisha. Only then did he open his eyes, fixing them on Jehoshaphat. "Make this valley full of ditches." The kings looked at one another in consternation, then back to Elisha, who was speaking. "For this is what the Lord says: You will see neither wind nor rain, yet this valley will be filled with water, and you, your cattle, and your other animals will drink. This is an easy thing in the eyes of the Lord; he will also hand Moab over to you. You will overthrow every fortified city and every major town. You will cut down every good tree, stop up all the springs, and ruin every good field with stones."

The kings left the tent and conferred briefly. "He speaks the oracles of God!" one of them exclaimed. Immediately they issued orders to carry out Elisha's instructions. By nightfall shallow ditches crisscrossed the porous limestone alongside the Dead Sea.

All night long Gehazi listened for the sound of rain that might fill the ditches. Hearing none, his curiosity got the better of him, and in the wee hours of the morning he slipped out of the tent and went to investigate. Pack animals were down at the ditches slaking their thirst! Remarkably, the ditches were filled with water! Gehazi wasted little time drinking himself, then ran to alert the soldiers.

While the men were running to see for themselves, Gehazi hurried to tell the prophet. "Elisha, wake up! Water's coming from the way of Edom. The ditches are full! It must've rained somewhere—this must be flash flooding."

Sleepily, Elisha asked, "Did you hear any sounds of rain?"

"No," he admitted. "Could water from the Salt Sea seep through the porous rock?"

"The water comes from God, Gehazi. I do not concern

myself with how." With that, Elisha rolled over and went back to sleep.

Long after the prophet was snoring, Gehazi lay awake trying to figure out what had happened. Possible explanations kept coming to mind. *There could be underground springs,* he reasoned.

After some time Gehazi dozed off. When he woke up again Elisha was leaning over him. "Quiet," he cautioned, and beckoned the servant to follow.

Outside, the camp was quiet all around, the troops having fallen asleep again. Elisha pointed in the direction of clumps of cacti outlined against the horizon. "There's a man out there hiding behind a cactus."

Gehazi knew what that meant. "A Moabite spy."

Elisha agreed.

They watched the cactus for some time, but the Moabite did not move from the protective covering. Daylight was beginning to show in the eastern sky, and as they watched the desert dawn became as red as a sunset.

In a few minutes they saw the Moabite leave concealment, bending low and slipping away.

When he was out of sight Elisha said, "We might as well go back to bed. The men are tired and since they have no battle orders, they'll not be up soon."

They had not fallen asleep again before they became aware of a lot of people talking. At first Elisha thought they must be the soldiers, but then he realized the talk was coming from beyond the camp and was coming nearer. He got up, looked outside, and saw the Moabites approaching from the east. "Gehazi, run! Tell the commanders the Moabites are coming!"

Elisha sought out the officers who were observing the approaching troops from the shelter of an outcropping. "They must be drunk," the captain said.

"Sh-h-h. Let them get closer," Elisha said. "They must think we've abandoned camp."

"They're not marching," the captain observed. "They act as if they're going to a frolic."

When the Moabites drew within bowshot, the captains blew their trumpets and the allied troops spilled out of hiding, yelling battle cries! Taken by surprise, the Moabites fled every which way, the men of Israel, Judah, and Edom hot on their heels.

During the battle that followed a spy was captured and brought back to the allied camp. Elisha listened as a captain questioned him. The frightened man explained, "We saw this place a bloody battlefield." Terrified, he looked from one face to another pleading for mercy. "How were we to know there was water here? Believe me . . . it's never been here before . . . I know, I've lived near here . . . we thought . . . But it wasn't blood—it was only the sun reflecting on the water."

"What fools!"

"Fools we are, sir," the Moabite admitted, "but what were we to think? . . . I beg your pardon . . . the only thing we could figure out . . . your three forces had turned against each other . . . mutinied, something like that . . . turned against each other. It's not uncommon, you know, allies fighting among themselves . . . Knowing you to be valiant warriors all, we thought that you had fought to the finish . . . You quite agree, sir . . . such a slaughter of men and animals would fill this plain with blood. . . . The sun reflecting on the water looked for all the world like pools of blood . . . you've waded battlefields before—up to ankles in blood."

The interrogators were intrigued with his story.

"I saw this field with my own eyes, sir . . ." the frightened man insisted. "Sir, no one could have convinced me that what I was seeing was water reflecting the sun. I would have wagered my life that it was a battlefield!"

"So what did you expect to find?"

The captive squirmed. "You know, sir . . . dead bodies."

"And you were going to loot our corpses?"

The man was too afraid to answer. A soldier kicked him.

"Take him away," the officer ordered, and to the other soldiers, "After them. Don't let one of 'em escape!"

Many hours later Gehazi was weary with waiting for the pursuing troops to return and fretted about the way things were. "They're all so bloodthirsty, these sons of Abraham. As for myself, I have no stomach for all this fighting. I'm a man of peace, and I long for a life of tranquility. As for other men, they're always marching off to battle or coming home maimed and wounded, glorying in victory or weeping over defeat. And what is gained? Nothing. Mothers are left bereaved of sons, children fatherless, wives become widows. Are there no righteous souls left? Where, may I ask, are all those seven thousand souls who have not bowed the knee to Baal? Who but you and I, Elisha? As for the sons of the prophets, well, they leave a lot to be desired."

Elisha listened, then asked quietly, "What would you do with peace if you had it, Gehazi?"

"Without an inheritance, what could I do? My brother cheated me out of an olive grove that rightfully should have come to me. I could make a fortune in olive oil. I dream of shipping oil to foreign lands along the Great Sea—for lighting homes, for cooking, as a foodstuff, for medicine, for making soap. At night I lie awake dreaming of my servants toiling in the groves gathering the crop, of my oxen turning the mill wheel extracting the oil from the olives, my ships in the harbor loaded with great vats of oil."

"I used to know a prophet who was in the olive oil business," Elisha said. "He was never rich but he provided for his family. He died some time ago. I really should visit his wife to see how she fares."

When the troops straggled back from battle, the news was mixed. They had pursued the enemy, destroyed towns, felled fruit trees, filled fields with stones, but the hill fortress of Kirhareseth remained standing. A commander reported, "King Mesha took refuge in Kirhareseth, and just as we were about to attack, he came out on the wall of the city in sight of all of us. With him was his son, his firstborn, heir to the Moabite throne. As we watched he sacrificed his boy to the god Chemosh. With his own hand he set fire to the bier on which his son lay. Mesha's desperation aroused the wrath of his people and we knew we were no match for them and their god so we fled as fast as we could."

"You fled from a heathen god?" Gehazi asked contemptuously.

A soldier grabbed him by the throat. "What do you know, you yellow-livered prophet? Where were you when we fought to save your hide?" Disgusted, he threw him to the ground and spit on him.

The commander seemed not to see the incident busying himself with dismissing the troops. Whooping and hollering, the soldiers packed up their gear and left for home.

Elisha and Gehazi were packing their things. "Must a man of God always suffer for his faith?" Gehazi whined.

Ignoring his question Elisha replied, "Come along, Gehazi, if you're going with me."

Together they returned to the other side of the sea to make the circuit of prophet colonies.

Along the way Elisha decided to visit the widow of the prophet who once sold oil. When they found her she was greatly distressed. A burly looking man with an ox cart stood in the shade of her fig tree, chains in his hands, as if waiting with unfinished business. The widow could hardly speak for the emotion that choked her. Speaking in a low voice so that the man would not overhear, she told Elisha, "Your servant, my husband, is dead, and you know that he revered the Lord.

But now his creditor is coming to take my two boys as slaves."

Elisha looked about for her sons and not seeing them, he did not ask where they were. "How can I help you?"

The woman was sobbing in her apron.

"Tell me," he asked gently, "what do you have in your house?"

Stifling her sobs, she whispered, "Your servant has nothing there at all except a little oil."

Elisha saw the boys peeking around the corner of the house, and he smiled at them. "Go around and ask all your neighbors for empty jars. Don't ask for just a few," he told her. "Then go inside and shut the door behind you and your sons. Pour oil into all the jars and, as each one is filled, put it to one side."

The man in the shade of the fig tree heard what Elisha said and a smirk curled his lips as he sat down to wait out the events. Gehazi drew Elisha aside and offered him a seat on a wooden bench.

All afternoon they sat watching the boys running in and out of the house carrying jars, jugs, pots—any kind of container they could borrow. Finally the door was shut, and soon Elisha began hearing squeals of delight, and he knew the woman was experiencing the miracle. In his mind's eye he could see her pouring oil from her small pot and the oil continuing to pour, filling one vessel after another. The clanging of pots, the sounds of happy voices, the peals of laughter went on for some time until, in late afternoon, Elisha heard the woman tell one of her sons, "Bring me yet another one."

"There is not a jar left," he answered.

Activity inside the house grew quieter. No doubt the woman was bustling about sealing jars, or wiping excess oil that had spilled down the sides or onto the floor. Elisha looked up just as the widow appeared in the doorway. Her face flushed, eyes shining, she asked, "All the jars are full. What shall I do now?"

"Go, sell the oil and pay your debts," he told her. "You and your sons can live on what is left." Elisha smiled back at her, then followed her gaze. The creditor threw the chains in the back of the cart. Picking up the goad he called out to the woman, "I'll be back tomorrow for my money."

"I'll have it by sundown," she promised.

The grateful boys flung themselves in Elisha's arms, hugging him. Elisha thought what he might give them and remembered two stones that would fascinate any child. "Here," he said, "I have something for you. Bring me my kit, Gehazi." The servant brought the kit and Elisha reached inside to find the two loadstones. "Do you know what these are?"

"No, what are they?"

"I'll show you." Elisha placed the stones at opposite ends and immediately they were attracted, attaching themselves as if glued. Turning them the other way, they repelled one another.

"It's magic!" one of the boys exclaimed.

"No, not magic. They're made that way," Elisha told them.

Gehazi took a few grains of iron filings from his pouch and showed the boys how the loadstone snatched the fragments from his hand. They were fascinated. "Will the stone lift anything?"

"Anything that's metal providing it isn't too heavy." Elisha said.

Elisha and Gehazi left the boys happily entertaining themselves, to go back to Jericho.

It was late in the afternoon when the two reached Jericho, and when they arrived a discussion was underway among the prophets. Some of the young prophets who were not married lived in a community house. "We're bursting at the seams," one of them told Elisha. "Many young men have joined us, impressed by the way God took our father Elijah. Elijah's preaching and teaching, as well as that of lesser prophets, has disillusioned them with the gods of their parents. The wonders God has performed by you and Elijah convince them that the unseen God is the living God." He glanced about the crowded room. "What we ought to do is enlarge our quarters."

"How?"

"Well, if each of us would go down to the river and cut one timber, we'd have enough to build another room."

"Sounds like a good idea," Elisha said. Knowing they had no money to hire servants to do the work, he wondered if they had the tools.

"Will you go with us?" one of them asked Elisha.

"Of course."

The next morning, the student prophets trooped down to the river with whatever tools they could beg or borrow, singing as they went. At the river they stopped long enough to convert their robes into trouser-like garments which were more suitable for physical work. This they did by bringing the robe between their legs and tucking it in their girdle or belt.

The work was going well when one of the men began having trouble—his axhead kept slipping. Quickly he kneeled down, fitting the helve back on the handle, securing it with wooden pegs wedged in between the iron and the wood. Satisfied that it was repaired, he went back to work cutting his tree.

The young men sweltered in the tropical heat, felling the trees, limbing them up, and hauling them to the building site. The woodcutter with the faulty ax swung with vigor. As he raised the ax high overhead and brought it down with the same powerful swing he'd been using all morning, the axhead flew off the handle, spun in the air, and landed in the Jordan! "Oh, my lord," he cried, "it was borrowed!"

"Go in after it," somebody yelled.

"There's nothing but mud down there," another said. "You'd never find it."

"Where did it fall?" Elisha asked.

"Right about there." The distressed man pointed to the middle of the river.

Gehazi was standing between Elisha and the man. "I know just the thing," he said. "Does anybody have a loadstone? A loadstone would bring the iron to the surface."

"There's no loadstone big enough to do that," he was told.

Elisha motioned his servant aside. Seeing where the man was pointing, he made a mental note, and going back from the stream he cut a low-hanging branch from a tree. Returning to the bank he tossed the stick in the water near the place where the iron had fallen. The stick drifted lazily on the slow current and, as they watched, they saw the axhead slowly rising to the surface! The young prophet's mouth dropped open. Smiling reassuringly, Elisha said, "Lift it out." And the prophet reached out and took the floating axhead.

"How'd he do that?" someone asked Gehazi.

"Elisha didn't do it," he replied, and walked away.

From Jericho, Elisha and Gehazi went to Gilgal. While they were there a man from Baalshalisha, a village thirteen miles distant, came bringing the first fruits of his harvest. The twenty barley loaves and grain in the husks were an offering to God commanded by the law.

Elisha took the offering, handed it to Gehazi, and told him, "Give it to the people to eat."

Gehazi protested, "How can I set this before a hundred men?"

"Give it to the people to eat. For this is what the Lord says, 'They will eat and have some left over.' "

Gehazi rolled his eyes as much as to say, "This is foolish." Laying the loaves before him in order, and the grain, he hesitated, not knowing what to do next. Elisha gave him the nod and, reluctantly, Gehazi began breaking the bread and passing it out to one person after another. The broken bread did not diminish! As long as they were eating, the bread did not give out nor did the cereal grains fail. When every man had consumed his share, there were still portions and scraps left over.

Elisha did not linger to enjoy their marveling nor to explain. These were dark days when unusual manifestations of God's love were needed. He had no other explanation.

As Elisha and Gehazi traveled about the countryside, they saw the effects of famine everywhere. Animals lay dead in the fields for lack of grazing land, children with swollen bellies begged in the streets, mothers were feeding their families unclean meat. Everyone was comparing this famine with the one during the life of Elijah. There were accusations that Elisha was responsible for present conditions, even as Elijah had been held responsible for the other. Elisha knew he did not cause the famine, he only predicted it.

One would think, Elisha said to himself, *that the three-and-a-half-year famine in Elijah's day would be sufficient to bring Israel to her senses, but it didn't.* Now that God had doubled the years of famine to seven Elisha wondered if the judgment would be any more effective than the first.

When Elisha and his servant came again to Gilgal they found the sons of the prophets hungry, with nothing to eat. He told Gehazi to set on a big pot and boil stew for them. Gehazi obeyed, and one of the men went out hoping to find something edible to cook. By chance he plucked a wild plant, and brought back a lap full of squash-like fruit. Slicing them into the pot he commented, "I don't know what they are, but they look good to me."

"Anything looks good when your stomach's empty," his friend replied.

"Wild cucumber?" someone suggested. "I hope it isn't colquintida! It'll give us the runs if it is."

The bubbling stew smelled good, and when Gehazi lifted the lid to stir it the vegetables were tender. "Shall I serve it now?" he asked, and in answer bowls were thrust in his face. Hungrily, the sons of the prophets were blowing on the hot pottage, ready to devour it. The first man to swallow suddenly turned white as a sheet! Dropping his dish, he stumbled away from the circle, wretching as he went. Elisha went after him just as he fell writhing on the ground, "O man of God, there is death in the pot!"

"Dump it out! Dump it out!" the men shouted.

"No!" Elisha ordered, and went back to the fire. "Get me some flour."

Taking the flour, he let it dribble through his fingers into the simmering stew. He waited a few minutes for the meal to take effect, then told them, "Serve it to the people to eat."

Wary at first, the sons of the prophets gingerly tasted the hot broth. Encouraged by the taste, they were emboldened to eat more. Famished as they were, they ate all of the stew and there were no ill effects.

Elisha moved about the country cautiously, for the Syrians were on the march as they were accustomed to be whenever they thought they had the advantage. Syria's king, Ben-hadad, in the secret confines of his strategic command headquarters, counseled with the finest military minds in his service to come up with tactics to outwit Israel. Painstakingly, they traced their maneuvers on maps, coded their commands to officers, and sent messages only by trusted couriers.

Nevertheless, the Syrians could never take Israel by surprise for the reason that God always revealed the plans to Elisha who, in turn, warned King Jehoram. Several times by this means Israel thwarted the battle plans of Syria.

Ben-hadad was enraged, thinking there must be a spy within Syrian ranks, and he accused his confidants. "Will you not tell me which of us is on the side of the king of Israel?" he asked.

And one of his servants answered, "None of us, my lord the king, but Elisha, the prophet who is in Israel, tells the king of Israel the very words you speak in your bedroom."

Immediately a contingent of fast-riding cavalrymen were dispatched to find out where the enemy was so that Ben-hadad could send men to capture him. They found Elisha at Dothan, and reported back to Damascus. A host of charioteers and infantrymen were sent by night to surround the town of Dothan and take Elisha captive.

The morning after this was done Elisha's servant got up early, and looking outside he saw the Syrian army with horses and chariots surrounding the city. Rushing to tell his master, Gehazi cried out in fear, "Oh, my lord, what shall we do?"

Elisha laid a hand on his servant's shoulder. "Don't be afraid. Those who are with us are more than those who are with them." Then the prophet lifted his face in prayer. "O Lord, open his eyes so he may see."

Elisha took Gehazi up on the roof of the house where they were staying, and as the young man stood looking at the Syrian host, the light of understanding broke in upon him. Elisha could see it in his face, and he knew the servant was seeing what he was seeing—the surrounding hills covered with horses and chariots of fire—angels protecting them.

"Come," Elisha said, "we'll go down and talk to these Syrian warriors!" No sooner did they appear in the courtyard than a Syrian captain came across the road. Elisha prayed, "Strike these people with blindness."

The captain came up to them, stated his business, and inquired about the whereabouts of one Elisha.

"This is not the road," Elisha answered, "and this is not the city. Follow me, and I will lead you to the man you are looking for."

The captain signaled his aide, explained the situation, and the word was passed. Elisha, riding on an old mule, was followed by his servant who, from time to time, cut the backsides of the animal with a switch. They took the lead and the Syrians followed them onto the road to Samaria, the capital of Israel.

Gehazi was astonished as, without a qualm, the Syrians fell in behind them. "What kind of 'blindness' is this that afflicts them?" he asked. "They're seeing but do not recognize us, the place, or landmarks. Perhaps they're in a state of walking in their sleep."

"Gehazi, do you remember the men of Sodom who wearied themselves in trying to find Lot's door?"

"I remember," Gehazi said, and the reminder served to reassure him that the same phenomenon might be happening again.

The mule was agile, even if old, and from time to time Elisha had to wait for the troops with their heavy equipment to catch up with them. As they were approaching the city watchmen saw them coming, reported it, and a number of militia came out to meet them. Elisha waved them aside and, getting down from the mule, he handed the reins to Gehazi and led the unsuspecting enemies through the gate. Merchants in the market stalls stood speechless as the Syrians filed past. Women and children crowded along the edge of the street, gawking in amazement at what they were seeing.

When the company reached the plaza in the center of town Elisha called a halt. Then the Lord opened the Syrians' eyes so that they realized they were in the midst of their enemies.

King Jehoram came out to the plaza and was flabbergasted at the sight of the terrified Syrians trembling in the street. As cynical as he was, he could not deny what his eyes were seeing. Rushing down to Elisha he asked the prophet, "Shall I kill them, my father? Shall I kill them?"

"Do not kill them. Would you kill men you have captured with your own sword or bow? Set food and water before them so that they may eat and drink and then go back to their master."

The cleverness of the strategy appealed to Jehoram. "Ah,

yes. Ben-hadad will be astonished by the story his men will tell. You think he will be afraid of such supernatural power and refrain from attacking us again."

The strategy had its desired result. For some time Syria stopped making raids on Israel.

Previously, on one such raid a small band of Syrian soldiers had swooped down the Golan Heights and taken what they could of plunder and slaves. Among the slaves was an Israelite girl. A very young girl, she was put in the service of the wife of Naaman, a high-ranking officer in the Syrian army. Naaman had distinguished himself by repelling an Assyrian assault, and for this he was accorded the honor of being prime minister to King Ben-hadad.

But Naaman contracted leprosy, that dreaded disease that progressively debilitates. Understanding that her master was afflicted with the disease, the slave girl told her mistress, "If only my master would see the prophet who is in Samaria! He would cure him of his leprosy."

Naaman's wife told him what the girl had said. Perhaps Elisha's exploits were well known to Naaman, or perhaps desperation drove him to speak about it to Ben-hadad. In any event Ben-hadad wrote a letter to King Jehoram of Israel requesting that his officer be healed.

Naaman assembled an impressive retinue, officers of rank and servants in great numbers. The gifts he chose were in keeping with his position—ninety-six pounds of gold, plus silver and costly garments. Then, with Ben-hadad's letter in hand, the caravan began its six-day journey from Damascus to Samaria.

Elisha heard of Namaan's visit not from King Jehoram, but from travelers who encountered the caravan on the road. Later he heard that King Jehoram had torn his clothes in response to the letter Naaman brought him, for he considered the request impossible. "Am I God?" he exploded. "Can I kill and bring back to life?" And, characteristic of his pessimistic nature, Jehoram thought Ben-hadad was looking for an excuse to invade Israel. "Why does this fellow send someone to me to be cured of his leprosy? See how he is trying to pick a quarrel with me!"

Elisha sent one of the sons of the prophets from Jericho with a word to Jehoram. "Why have you torn your robes? Have the man come to me and he will know that there is a prophet in Israel."

Patiently, Elisha waited. He had never been used to heal a man of leprosy before, but God had told him what to tell Naaman, and Elisha was confident the man would be healed. From his house in Jericho Elisha saw the cavalcade coming— the princely figures mounted upon swaying camels, the string of asses bearing the baggage, some servants on foot and others handling the reins of teams pulling wagons. He knew it had been a tiring ordeal for Naaman, sick as he was, climbing over the hill of Ephraim and down the steep pass that led to Gilgal. Feeling sorry for him, Elisha was tempted to go out to meet him; but he restrained himself. It would not do to have Naaman think God's prophet was unduly pleased or honored by his visit. He sat still in the house as Naaman was knocking at his gate. Sending his servant to the gate, he gave him this message for Naaman. "Go wash yourself seven times in the Jordan, and your flesh will be restored to you and you will be clean."

The message delivered, Elisha could hear loud expostulations coming from the courtyard. Storming out, Naaman shouted, "I thought that he would surely come out to me and stand and call on the name of the Lord his God, wave his hand over the spot and cure me of my leprosy." The sick man, still raging, was being helped back onto his horse. "Are not Abana and Pharpar, the rivers of Damascus, better than any of the waters of Israel?" he yelled. "Couldn't I wash in them and be cleansed?" He dug his spurs in the sides of the horse, but a servant holding the reins restrained him.

Elisha could hear the servants pleading with Naaman. "My father, if the prophet had told you to do some great thing, would you not have done it? How much more then when he tells you, 'Wash, and be cleansed'?"

Naaman's resistance faltered. His weary body slumped, his head dropped down on his chest. In a little while he threw his leg over the back of his mount and, without a word, slid to the ground. Striding toward the river he walked straight into the water until he was waist deep, then ducked down, submerging his whole body. Coming up, he wiped water from his face and eagerly examined his diseased flesh. Disappointed that he could find no improvement, he nevertheless went under the water again. Coming up the second time, he felt the eruptions on his forehead and found no change in his condition. Without hesitating, he took a third plunge, anxious to get the matter over with. When there was yet again no healing, Naaman looked as if he might give up; but seeing his anxious servants entreating him to try again, he did.

But it was not until Naaman had bathed the seventh time that he was healed. When he came up out of the water and felt of his forehead, his nose, and ears—there was no sign of leprosy! As he examined his fingers, the backs of his hands, his forearms, thighs, his toes, he saw that his flesh was as healthy as that of a little child! Splashing his way to shore, so happy his face was shining, he was so ecstatic he couldn't speak. The excited servants quickly dried him and helped him dress, laughing and crying at the same time.

The happy company returned to Elisha's house with their grateful master, and found the prophet waiting at the gate for them. His eyes brimming with tears, his voice trembling, Naaman embraced Elisha. "Now I know that there is no God in all the world except in Israel. Please accept now a gift from your servant." Naaman beckoned to a servant to fetch the gifts.

Gehazi helped the men bring the pile of goods and lay them at the prophet's feet. Elisha's servant could not keep his eyes off the magnificent clothing, the sacks of gold and silver. Elisha shook his head emphatically. "As surely as the Lord lives, whom I serve, I will not accept anything." He could not take pay for what God had done. *Besides,* he reasoned, *if Naaman pays a price, he will feel he owes no gratitude.*

"Please, sir," the Syrian urged him, but Elisha was adamant. Then Naaman said, "If you will not, please let me, your servant, be given as much earth as a pair of mules can carry, for your servant will never again make burnt offerings and sacrifices to any other god but the Lord."

Elisha granted the request, understanding that the earth from Gilgal was as sacred to Naaman as the territory of the unseen, living God, whereas the soil of Syria belonged to idols. Granted the request, Naaman had another to make; and when he spoke his voice was so grave it quavered. "But may the Lord forgive your servant for this one thing: When my master enters the temple of Rimmon to bow down and he is leaning on my arm and I bow there also—when I bow down in the temple of Rimmon, may the Lord forgive your servant for this."

Elisha smiled benevolently. The act was one of duty, not allegiance. "Go in peace, Naaman."

All the company was bowing in respect for Elisha, and he returned their courtesy. Naaman mounted his stallion, and looking down at Elisha saluted him, then turned back on the road. For a few minutes Elisha stood at the gate watching the departing cavalcade, then went back in the house.

Gehazi remained in the courtyard. Instinct told Elisha that Gehazi's lingering interest in the visitors bode no good. Long after the horses' hoofs no longer sounded in his ear, Elisha waited for Gehazi to come inside. When he did not return, the prophet realized his servant had followed after the troupe. It did not take him long to understand why. *I should have known,* he thought, *when I saw Gehazi lusting over the gifts Naaman was offering me. . . . I wonder what story he concocted to get Naaman to give him something.*

Near the time for the evening sacrifice Gehazi slipped back to the house and tiptoed up the outside steps to his room above. Elisha listened. He heard a scraping sound . . . a lid being raised . . . something being dragged across the floor.

After a little while Gehazi came downstairs and entered Elisha's room. His manner was unusually cheerful, and when Elisha asked him where he had been he replied, "Your servant didn't go anywhere."

The lie outraged Elisha. "Was not my spirit with you when the man got down from his chariot to meet you? Is this the time to take money, or accept clothes"—his voice rose higher with indignation—"olive groves, vineyards, flocks, herds, or menservants and maidservants?"

Gehazi, full of arrogance, stiffened, a contemptuous grin on his face. Elisha looked at him with pity and, speaking in a coarse whisper, told him, "Naaman's leprosy will cling to you and to your descendants forever."

The arrogance not lessening, the grin unchanged, Gehazi turned on his heel and left. Elisha heard him taking the steps two at a time. Overhead, in his room, Gehazi was scrambling about, retrieving whatever it was Naaman had given him. In a few minutes he rushed downstairs again, burst into the room, and held out the loot—a wedge of gold, a bag of silver, and priestly robes. He shook them at the prophet, laughed a mirthless laugh, and clutching the ill-gotten gain to his chest, laughed again.

Elisha turned his back on him. The door slammed. Gehazi was gone.

4

Jonah

J onah, sitting on the fringe of the sons of the prophets, had a decision to make. In his heart of hearts he had already made the decision but, as his nature was, he was going through the process of giving reasons to himself if not to God.

The men were talking about Elisha, remembering his exploits, caught up in vicarious fantasies of their own. In his youth Jonah had aspired to follow in the footsteps of Elisha but, alas, the mantle had fallen upon no one, and there was not a man among them who had performed a miracle in the manner of Elisha. Hounded by their persecutors, prophets spent most of their time trying to stay alive, and they had little influence on Israelite society.

Jonah was for keeping the status quo. True, corruption and injustice marked the regime, but prospects for peace had never been better. Ammon—in fact all of the Arabs to the east and the Philistines to the west—had been subdued. Since Assyria's attack on Damascus Israel had enjoyed relief from her Syrian neighbor; and King Ashurnirari of Assyria, though strong enough to maintain a powerful nation, was too weak to wage wars of aggression.

Jonah did not like even to hear the name *Assyrian,* for it flooded his mind with stories of their atrocities. Not content to kill their victims they tortured, mutilated, dismembered, flayed alive, boiled, and impaled them! Threatened by advancing Assyrian troops, entire villages had committed suicide.

To Jonah God's command that he go to Nineveh—the capital of Assyria—and warn them of coming destruction was outrageous. *I know what will happen if I go there,* he told himself. *To save their hides they'll repent. And, if I know God at all, I know he is merciful; he'll forgive them and we'll be right back where we started from. Why doesn't he simply judge them, destroy Nineveh, and rid the world of the threat to peace? If they must have the message, why doesn't God send it to them by some other means, why must I take it personally? That's a long and dangerous journey. No, God insists that I "go to the great city of Nineveh," as if there's no time to waste.*

The sons of the prophets were singing a Psalm as they always did when they were together. Jonah listened to hear if they got the words right. If there was anything he loved more than the Torah, it was the psalms of David and Asaph; yet when the prophets asked him to sing he declined.

"Why so melancholy?" a red-bearded youth asked him.

Someone laughed. "Jonah's always in a mood of one kind or another, aren't you, Jonah?"

He did not answer.

"Erratic, I'd say," the man continued, needling him. "On again, off again. Up one day, down the next."

Jonah felt his jaw harden. The fool made him sound unstable.

The young man defended him. "How can you say such things about a man who's served his country as Jonah has? Who else has predicted our recovery of all the territory taken from Israel? He stands in well with the king and that helps us all."

The others agreed and looked approvingly at Jonah.

As he thought about their confidence in him, Jonah knew that if he went to Nineveh he could never look them in the face again. Not only would his fellow prophets look upon him as a traitor, the king might very well execute him. Even if he escaped that, if his prophecy about Nineveh being destroyed in forty days did not come true, he would be discredited as a man of God.

Jonah stood up, tucked up his flowing robe in his girdle. "Where're you going?" the red-bearded one asked.

"To Joppa," he replied. The decision was made. No more sleepless nights; he would leave Israel, abandon his calling, and escape the command of God.

"That's fifty miles away. Why Joppa?"

Jonah did not answer.

The fifty miles seemed endless despite the steady gait of the ass he rode. They had traveled all night and Jonah was so tired he thought he could not ride another mile. As they finally came in sight of the harbor, Jonah remembered Djehuti, the Egyptian general who had won a great victory at Joppa and how the credit was given to Amun-Re, king of gods. It concerned Jonah that God's people had never claimed the city, though they used the port as their gateway to the Sea.

Jonah stopped and surveyed the harbor, hoping to find a vessel. Among the small craft there was one handsome Phoenician ship idling dockside, its splendid masts standing tall in the morning sun, its three-tiered oars at rest. "Oh, I hope I can get passage on that one!" He touched his heels to the donkey's sides, and the animal started ambling down the slope.

Crewmen were going up and down the gangplank loading cargo. *Olive oil, no doubt,* Jonah thought, *maybe wine. There's no telling what they brought with them—dye, for sure; probably cedar and wool . . . I wonder where they're going. Of course, it really doesn't matter . . . It looks as if they might be weighing anchor soon.*

A slow-moving barge bearing timbers was easing down the coast, a small fishing skiff was heading out to sea. The smell of salt in the air and the mewing of gulls lifted his spirits. He was indeed getting away from it all.

When he reached the pier Jonah had trouble finding the shipmaster, and once he found him the man was too busy to listen to his request. Jonah watered the ass, tethered it to a tree where there was some grass to graze. Then, exhausted, he sat down on a pile of tackling where he could keep an eye on the pilot and watch the seamen working. He kicked at a cur dog that was sniffing at him, and asked one of the workmen where the ship was bound.

"Tarshish and every port between," he was told.

That's good, he thought. *That's as far away as I can get,* and he began plotting in his head where the ship might stop for ports of call along the way. *Let's see, they'll travel south and west along Egypt's coast . . . then Cyrene . . . Tarshish is at the mouth of some river . . . what's the name of that river . . .* In a little while he gave up. He was so tired his brain wouldn't work. Still . . . *Never mind,* he thought.

"Where are you going?" a sailor asked.

"I flee the presence of God." The seaman shrugged his shoulders and kept on working, hauling hides aboard, dumping them in the hold.

A babel of languages sounded in Jonah's ears, few of which he identified, and the smells that assaulted his senses were as equally overwhelming. The rancid stench of the hides mingled with the smells of sweat and urine; fishy-smelling flotsam floating in the water attracted scavenger birds and flies that swarmed about his face. The flea-bitten cur would not leave him alone although he slapped at it. Lying at his feet, it whined and thumped its tail against the dock. Jonah sighed despairingly. Every bone in his body cried out for sleep.

Some of the sailors were checking the ropes, readying the vessel to sail, and from inside the ship came the clanking of chains and shouted curses. *Slaves,* he guessed. Phoenicians were notorious for pirating passengers, sailing away, and selling them as slaves in foreign ports. Jonah would not allow himself to think about that—he didn't need anything else to worry about.

A richly dressed merchant—silk turban adorning his head, gold embroidery embellishing his coat, and pantaloons in the fashionable style of the East—boarded the ship, his servants following, carrying chests of his personal belongings. They were followed by a slave pulling two reluctant goats onto the gangplank.

The cur had sidled alongside Jonah and was panting its foul breath in his face. Jonah groaned, turned the other way, slapped at the pests annoying him, and prayed the ship would soon get underway. To occupy his mind he studied the tiers of oars carved from oak. Sailors were beginning to man them. Crewmen had cleared the dock and were getting on board. Suddenly he realized he may be left, and jumping up he yelled at the shipmaster. "Sir!"

The pilot turned around. Jonah ran toward him, the dog at his heels. "How much is the fare to Tarshish?"

The captain eyed him shrewdly. Seeing that he had no baggage, he must have guessed Jonah was a fugitive. With a sardonic smile he told him the sum.

Jonah paid the fare and went to fetch his donkey.

"We've no room for the ass," the man told him. "Sell it. You'll buy better in Tarshish."

Jonah frantically raced about trying to find someone to buy the ass. The cur, thinking it a frolic, leaped up and bounced about, tripping Jonah not once but twice! Seeing a bargeman, Jonah called out, "Can you use a good donkey?"

"If it's free."

Jonah could see the crew was taking in the gangplank. "Take it," he yelled, and jumping over the dog he ran to the pier, took a running leap, and barely landed on the deck. "Whew!" he exclaimed. Looking back he saw the cur on the dock nervously considering whether or not to attempt the jump. "Go back! Go back!" Jonah shouted, and as the ship steadily moved away, the dog put its head between its front paws and whined after him.

Once aboard the vessel Jonah wanted nothing more than to find a place to sleep; but the pompous merchant, seeing the loss Jonah took on the donkey, was full of advice. A talkative man, he would not let him go. Motioning to a bench near the bulkhead he introduced himself as a silk merchant from Borsippa, and they sat down. As the ship moved quietly out of the harbor, the oars swishing in rhythmic concert and the city receding from view, the Babylonian bored Jonah with facts about who he was, where he came from, where he was going, how much he owned, and how famous he was. When he asked Jonah about himself, Jonah said only that he was a Hebrew, and thought to himself that by comparison to this man the sad-eyed dog on the pier was not such a bad companion after all.

When the ship cleared the harbor seamen unfurled the sails, and the Babylonian marveled at the beauty of them. "Egyptian linen, I wager."

Jonah was not interested in anything the man had to say; but one of the mariners overheard the comment, and when his work was done he joined the conversation. "We build the finest ships in the sea," he boasted. "This one's a beauty, ain't she?"

"Look yonder, man!" the Babylonian exclaimed, pointing.

Three sea creatures had simultaneously leaped out of the water and dived down again. The mariner was not excited by the sight. "I've seen 'em leap thataway, turn a somersault in the air. Keep watching, ye'll see 'em come up again." And no sooner had he spoken than it happened.

Other sailors joined them and watched the antics until the creatures were out of sight. Among the seamen was a lad of no more than twelve years. "Tell us more," he asked, and the old mariner was pleased to oblige. "The sea is full of them kind and others, lad. There's bigger ones comes up for air then down again. Monsters they are, too. I've seen 'em with me own eyes—dragons bigger 'n any ship ye'll ever see, with long necks and tails and bodies big as to house this whole crew."

"Have you no fear?" the merchant asked.

"Aye, no. We stay close by the coast unless, of course, a storm blows us off course—and, in that case, I've still no fear, for the stars control the sea and all that's in them." He tapped a crude medallion, etched with a constellation of stars, that hung about his neck on a leather cord. "This here'll keep me safe."

"You've seen dragons—sea monsters?"

"Many's the time. And I've heard from other men things you won't believe."

"Perhaps I will," the merchant said, egging him on.

The mariner squinted his eyes and drew closer to confide. "I've heard it more than once. Many times it's been told me, in more ports than one. Me mates here will bear me out. There was once a leviathan thrown up on a beach of Chittim, some say Marea—and when they cut the monster open—for it has a fine oil—inside the belly was a horse swallowed whole!"

The silk merchant laughed, but the mariners were in earnest, agreeing that the story was true. Their weatherbeaten faces, though grimey from their chores, showed scars from many a brawl and battle. Jonah judged that they were not worthy men and chose not to believe them.

"Aye, he tells the truth," one of them said. "Do we not all know well how them monsters, in time of danger, swallow their young, then spit them out again? Perhaps he done the same for the horse only he couldn't get him up again!" They roared laughing.

The boy was playing with a cat that lay sleepily in his arms, uninterested in his teasing. "What ails ye, Anatolia?" he asked.

"Don't you know, lad, what good omen that cat gives ye? There's fair weather up ahead. Now if the weather be foul she'd be telling the shipmaster with the arch of her back and a hissing to make 'im know."

"Are you afraid of storms?" the boy asked.

"A storm?" He laughed. "Stout seamen laugh at gales."

"What about leviathans?"

"Well," he answered, scratching the stubble of his beard, "That's another matter. There's men standing here that knows I'm telling the truth. Once there was a man clad in full armor found inside one of them leviathans. Oh, they has jaws, them monsters—six feet across or more. I'd not like to be in the water with one o' them!"

"Jaws, yes, and a blow hole for air," a skinny, tattooed seaman added. "They come up out of the water, blow and snort like a stallion, then go below again."

The Babylonian, not to be outdone, spoke up, "We have an ancient tradition in my part of the world, one believed for generations, that a half-fish, half-man came out of the sea, a veritable god who taught our people crafts and skills."

"Aye, I've heard that tale as well," the tattooed one said.

Jonah, not wishing to get into a religious discussion, slipped away from the group and went below deck. There he found a place between some sacks of grain where he could lie down. In minutes he was sound asleep.

Just how long he slept he never knew. He was in a stupor when the pilot shook him awake, shouting, "How can you sleep?" The look on the man's face was more astonishment than anger. For a moment Jonah didn't know what he was talking about, then he realized the ship was heaving up and down sending sacks of grain sailing. *Where's the rest of the cargo?* he wondered, but the shipmaster was yelling something he couldn't hear above the crack of thunder. Drenching wet, the pilot's face was white with alarm as he screamed, "Get up and call on your god! Maybe he will take notice of us, and we will not perish." With that he went reeling across the littered deck, the ship lurching violently.

Jonah tried to get to his feet but was thrown down. On hands and knees he crawled to the hatchway and climbed the slippery ladder. As soon as his head poked through the hatch fierce wind and rain assaulted him. In a flash of lightning he saw the boy lashed to a mast, terror in his eyes, crying out to the gods. The other seamen and the merchant, clinging to a cable and crouching down behind the bulkhead, were crying out frenzied prayers. Seeing Jonah, they reached out and pulled him into the huddle. The ship, rolling in the sea, waves washing over the deck, seemed doomed. When the shipmaster climbed out from below the drenched sailors threw him one end of the cable and he pulled himself toward them hand over hand, crawling on his belly. Shouting above the shrieking wind and lashing rain, he told them, "We're going to cast lots to see who's responsible."

"Responsible?" Jonah asked.

"It's no ordinary storm! Somebody on this ship has brought this evil upon us. We've a murderer—a thief aboard!"

A murderer, a thief—there must be a dozen or more on board, thought Jonah, and he wondered at their stupidity.

The shipmaster was putting counters in a bottle with a narrow neck, one for each man aboard. The gale, like a restive beast, slackened; but before they could fill the bottle with water it came full force again, blowing the water away as it poured. Moving closer together, the sailors shielded the bottle with their bodies so that when the wind slackened again they were able to fill it. The shipmaster motioned for them to bring the boy.

Two seamen, holding onto each other and a secure rope, fought their way to the mast, lightning crackling, wind moaning. Unloosing the frightened youth they brought him, slipping and sliding across the deck, to where the others were. Handing the boy the bottle, they told him to close his eyes then pour out the counters one at a time. By the order in which each man's counter came, guilt was determined.

The lot fell upon Jonah!

The shipmaster and all the sailors looked aghast. They did not believe the lot! The shipmaster peered inside the bottle; seeing nothing, he shook it. Dismayed, he turned to Jonah and bombarded him. "Tell us who is responsible for making all this trouble? What do you do? Where do you come from? What is your country? From what people are you?"

Cupping his hands to his mouth to make himself heard, he yelled, "I am a Hebrew and I worship the Lord, the God of heaven, who made the sea and land."

The men stared at him, horrified. "What have you done?"

Jonah didn't answer. He had told them before he was running away from the Lord.

He could see on their faces the question in their minds, 'If you fear the Lord, why are you running away from him?'

The storm lashed out furiously and the ship could not right itself. Listing dangerously, they could feel the ship taking water below.

The shipmaster shouted, "What should we do to you to make the sea calm down for us?"

Jonah hesitated, then in one heroic move he told them, "Pick me up and throw me into the sea and it will become calm." A mountainous wave washed over the deck, nearly sending them overboard. Panic-stricken, Jonah confessed, "I know that it is my fault that this great storm has come upon you."

The sailors shook their heads at one another, finding it hard to believe. Jonah thought he understood one of them to say something about his being a decent man. It was plain to see they didn't want to lay hands on him.

"Let's try rowing again," one of them shouted. Hanging onto the cable, they were able to make their way to rowing positions and took up the futile task again. Jonah knew rowing wouldn't help, but while they were trying, he went below deck where he wedged himself in a corner, wrapped his arms around his knees and shivered from nerves and fear. *God knows I don't want to die . . . they're afraid to throw me overboard . . . I'd bail water if it would do any good.* Teeth chattering, dreading the watery grave, he grieved. *I'm not ready to meet my Judge.*

The shrill wind was tossing the vessel this way and that,

sending wave after wave over its sides. Jonah shook uncontrollably as he prayed over and over again that he might live, knowing full well that if the storm kept up they would all perish.

The rowers were getting nowhere, their oars waving out of the water as much as in. The shipmaster came below and shook his head at Jonah, as much as to say, "Why don't you jump?" He turned to the rowers and ordered a halt. Jonah came halfway up from the floor, frantic to escape, but sank down again, shaking like a leaf. The men were all praying at once, but they were not calling out the names of their own gods—they were calling out the name of Jehovah! "O Lord, please do not let us die for taking this man's life. Do not hold us accountable for killing an innocent man, for you, O Lord, have done as you pleased."

Jonah pressed himself against the wall; lips dry, he could hardly breathe! The sailors took hold of him, pinned his arms behind his back, and carried him kicking and screaming up the hatch ladder.

Once on deck they stopped a moment and gave Jonah time to pray or do whatever he wished. Jonah saw the churning cauldron below and shut his eyes. They were lifting him off his feet—swinging him back and forth to heave him well over the side—! Suddenly, they let go—he felt himself sailing through the air. Plummeting downward, the surging sea rose swiftly to swallow him. Sinking like a stone, helplessly kicking, thrashing about, the sea carried him this way and that! Lungs bursting, he felt himself being sucked in by some strong force. Darkness engulfed him.

When Jonah came to he was in a daze. Numbly he realized he was breathing! *Am I alive or dead?* he wondered. In the pitch darkness he could see nothing. Constant motion was rolling him about in the narrow confines of his prison. A noise like a horse blowing through its nostrils, and a chilling rush of air, more fully aroused him. Sensing he was trapped, Jonah panicked. "Where am I?" he cried out.

Only the swish of fluids answered him.

"I've got to get out of here!" he screamed, but he couldn't get to his feet nor keep any kind of balance. Grappling to catch hold of something, he was repeatedly carried upward, plunged downward, slipping and sliding. An oily substance, slippery and slimey, covered him.

It's no use, he thought. Exhausted, he sank back into oblivion.

For some time Jonah was in and out of consciousness and lay limp and helpless in the dark, wet chamber. After a while, for some reason, there was less motion, and he was able to lie in one cramped position hardly moving at all. In a rhythmic pattern of movement he was continually carried upward then down again. At the peak of the climb he would hear the shuddering, blowing sound and feel the rush of air. Unconsciously Jonah became accustomed to the pattern and braced himself accordingly. Once he sneezed, and when he did he realized seaweed was wrapped around his body, his face.

When he became more lucid Jonah heard himself laughing crazily. "Alive! I'm alive!" and laughing still, he could not stop.

After some time the hysteria lessened. Hours passed. A sense of well-being came over him. Bits and pieces of Psalms began coming to mind. *God is not cruel,* he told himself. *He will not leave me to die a torturous death. This leviathan—this angel— whatever it is carrying me about, God will deliver me, bring me back to the land of the living.*

Thinking back, he remembered his prayer aboard ship. And though at the time he had no faith it would be answered, he realized it was being answered, it definitely was! He gave voice to the thought.

In my distress I called to the Lord,
and he answered me.

From the depths of the grave I called
   for help,
and you listened to my cry.

Picking at the slimey seaweed he remembered the night-
mare of sinking in the water, and he thought of a Psalm the
sons of Korah sang, one about the noise of waterspouts, waves,
and billows passing over:

> You hurled me into the deep,
>   into the very heart of the seas,
>   and the currents swirled about me;
> all your waves and breakers
>   swept over me.

Overwhelmed at the mercy of God toward him, Jonah felt
remorse. *Some day, perhaps soon,* he thought, *I'll be able to pray
properly, looking toward the temple in Jerusalem.*

For some time he carefully put words together in his head
before he prayed them:

> I said: I have been banished
>   from your sight;
> yet I will look again
>   toward your holy temple.
> The engulfing waters threatened me,
>   the deep surrounded me;
>   seaweed was wrapped around my head.

His prayer was interrupted by the sudden cavorting of his
host, which threw Jonah about. As the sea creature righted
itself, the snorting reverberated in the chamber. A painful
cramp gripped the calf of Jonah's leg and he grabbed it in both
hands. As he massaged the leg he remembered the panic he had
felt as he was sinking to the bottom of the sea, buried by
mountains of waves and water. As he kneaded the muscle, he
talked to God.

To the roots of the mountains I sank
   down;
the earth beneath barred me in
   forever.
But you brought up my life from the pit,
   O Lord my God.

The knot of pain in his leg was subsiding, and Jonah stretched it as best he could and lay back again feeling nauseous. Despite feeling ill, despite being isolated as he was, Jonah did not feel alone. *I know I've been heard,* he told himself. *And I know I'm being heard now.*

When my life was ebbing away,
   I remembered you, Lord,
and my prayer rose to you,
   to your holy temple.

He reproached himself. *I wonder that I ever thought I could get away with this. Running away from God is ridiculous. If he let me go I could not have survived. A man who runs away from the Lord forsakes the only One who can help him, show him mercy.*

Those who cling to worthless idols
   forfeit the grace that could be theirs.

He stretched the leg again. *I'll never run away again,* he vowed. *Once I get out of here, I'll offer my sin offering and make proper thanksgiving for my forgiveness. I'll also do what he tells me to do, keep my vows. He's my salvation.* And Jonah spoke his resolutions to God.

But I, with a song of thanksgiving,
   will sacrifice to you.
What I have vowed I will make good.
   Salvation comes from the Lord.

Caught unaware, Jonah was turned upside down and felt violent contortions as the sea monster thrashed about. Each time the animal heaved Jonah felt himself jerked forward. Before he grasped what was happening, he was hurtled into the air!

Jonah landed hard, face down in the surf. Dazed, he lay there, his eyes dazzled by the sun. Before he could pick himself up excited people were rushing to help him. "He's alive! He's alive!" they shouted. Strong arms lifted him and carried him onto the beach. "Bring me some wine!" someone shouted.

Jonah nearly strangled as they poured wine in his mouth. Next they were loading him onto a litter, and Jonah could not stop the darkness engulfing him.

Jonah woke up later and found himself lying on a mat inside a house. His head was hurting and the light bothered his eyes. People jammed the room, staring at him in awesome silence. A woman was holding a bowl of hot broth ready to serve him. Jonah felt clean and dry. And, yes, hungry.

He slowly sat up, drank the broth, and waved aside their questions. He could hear gulls overhead. *This must be Joppa*, he thought. There was a stir in the crowd and looking up, Jonah saw the shipmaster coming toward him. White as a ghost, the man stared at him speechless.

Jonah smiled. "You got the vessel back to port?"

"The sea was calmed as soon as we—" He fumbled awkwardly. "Without a cargo, there was no reason to go on. We turned back."

"How long ago was that?"

"Three days, sir," and he bowed before him.

"Get up, man," Jonah said, irritated, his head pounding.

"Surely you have the oracles of God," he whispered.

"Nonsense!"

No sooner had Jonah said the word than God spoke to his heart. "Go to the great city of Nineveh, and proclaim to it the message I give you."

Jonah winced. But remembering his promise he started to get up, and had them clear the room so he could dress. After dressing, his head felt better. Jonah went into town hoping to put together a few supplies. As he was crossing the road the bargeman came running up to him, the donkey in tow. "Your ass, sir, your ass," he said, bowing and scraping. Dropping the reins at Jonah's feet, he turned and fled as if he'd seen a ghost.

Jonah smiled and set about to inquire about travel to Nineveh.

The merchant from Borsippa, so carried away with the news of Jonah's survival, and ecstatic that Jonah was going to Nineveh, decided to return home and outfitted a caravan for that purpose. "I've made ample provision for you, sir," he told Jonah. "We'll leave at your convenience."

It was a long and tiresome journey, but Jonah felt safe in the company of the merchant and his attendants, and the merchant told him everything he needed to know about Nineveh and its environs.

After nearly a month's travel, Jonah was let off at the River Tigris, where Nineveh rose on the other side, but not before the merchant had introduced him to the boatman who would take him the rest of the way. "This is the Hebrew prophet, Jonah, son of Amittai, of the town of Gath-heper near Nazareth in Zebulon."

The boatman's eyes shot wide open.

"You've heard of him?"

"The man come alive from a fish's belly?"

The merchant nodded, and turned to Jonah. "Your fame precedes you. Word spreads like wildfire. They'll be expecting you. You're another god thrown up by a fish."

When at last Jonah came in sight of Nineveh, his heart was heavy as lead. The massive walls, a hundred feet high and thick enough for three chariots abreast to drive upon, were flanked by fifteen hundred towers, each two hundred feet high. Magnificent gates, guarded by winged bulls, were each dedicated to a god. *Why doesn't God destroy Nineveh,* he complained, *and let well enough alone? Why warn them?*

As he entered by the gate of the moon god Jonah felt uncomfortable, people were staring at him. Some of them shied away from him or eyed him inquisitively as they passed on the street.

From a temple came the singing of hymns to the gods and in the air was the scent of incense burning. A serpent charmer, sitting on the steps of the temple, made motions, offering to augur from the entrails of a goat for him. Then, recognizing Jonah, the charmer was terrified, snatched up his accoutrements, and fled.

Jonah sought the anonymity of the marketplace. Apparently a fair was going on, and he hoped he could lose himself in the crowd. Blue and purple awnings sheltered the wares from the sun's heat, and Jonah stood in the shadow of a Phoenician booth examining glass objects for sale. Like alabaster, the glass was smooth and opaque—small bottles and vases made from molds.

Every country was represented there—Tarshish with silver, tin, iron, and lead. *Tarshish,* he murmured to himself, as he handled the items displayed. The vendor, mistaking his interest, eagerly prattled in a foreign tongue trying to sell him something, and Jonah moved on.

Amid the confusion of hawkers shouting their wares, merchants haggling with buyers, Jonah expected to be unnoticed; yet, from time to time, strangers turned around to take a second look stopped in the street and pointed him out, talking excitedly. *I guess they've heard but don't quite know,* he reasoned.

The smell of spices was in the air, together with that of goat dung and human odors. Raw meat, swarming with flies, hung in the butcher's stall out of the way of stray dogs. Not knowing the language well, Jonah supplemented words with signs to buy a smoked fish. He ate the fish as he admired the Armenian horses, the famous Nisaean breed.

In the dust and heat Jonah had no heart for what he must do. Soon he must begin, but he loathed his mission.

A man eyed him curiously, recognizing his dress as that of a Hebrew, and was about to speak. Jonah quickly turned away. Ducking down a narrow passageway between the spread tents, he busied himself at the table of ivory from Arabia—horns, calamus, and cassia spread on display. The passageway was choked with women milling about, exclaiming over the precious stones, linen and embroidery from Syria. Men sniffed wine from Damascus and leered at the manacled slave women on the block. Jonah guessed the miserable captives were from Meshech.

He could delay no longer.

Shouting at the top of his lungs he cried, "Forty more days and Nineveh shall be destroyed!" The babel of voices was suddenly silenced. Every eye turned toward him. Jonah waited, surveying the sea of faces, their attention riveted on him. Then, shouting, he made his way through the crowd. "Forty more days and Nineveh shall be destroyed!"

People were visibly shaken. A message rippled through the crowd: "He's the one. That's Jonah, the man who was swallowed by the fish!" A woman fainted, another screamed. Anxious mothers called their children and, wailing, grabbed them up in their arms.

Jonah strode with an unrelenting pace through the city, a crowd following, weeping and wringing their hands. On the steps of every temple he proclaimed the doom, in every neighborhood, every side street. Crowds followed him, hour after hour, to all the plantations where he delivered the warning and to Calah.

As Jonah crossed the street in front of the king's palace, he saw the sculptured reliefs adorning the walls—battle scenes depicting the rain of arrows falling on Assyrian enemies, captives in chains, conquered kings made footstools. In the courtyard there were hunting scenes and banqueting scenes, and to Jonah all of it was revolting.

King Ashurnirari himself was waiting for Jonah at the end of a long, sloping hall. Clothed in black goat hair the king, having heard the warning, was already in mourning for the sins of Nineveh. An aide handed him a scroll, and when the crowd was hushed King Ashurnirari read the proclamation: "Let neither man nor beast, herd nor flock, taste anything; let them not feed, nor drink water. But let man and beast be covered with sackcloth, and cry mightily unto God; yea, let them turn every one from his evil way, and from the violence that is in their hands. Who can tell if God will turn and repent, and turn away from his fierce anger, that we perish not?"

In ceremonial dignity the king came down from his throne, and in view of the assembled crowd sat down in ashes. At the sight, people wept and wailed, beat their breasts and threw dust in the air. Jonah left them there and moved on, spreading the alarm.

The next day Jonah walked to outlying settlements where the king's proclamation preceded him, and the fast was underway. The result was astonishing. Everywhere he went the Assyrians were conscience stricken—sitting in ashes, dressed in sackcloth, raising a tumult with their mourning. Farm animals were lowing for want of water and feed.

As he walked back through Nineveh he found the fair abandoned, the royal harnass horses draped in sackcloth. People swarmed after him so that he scarce could breathe. Jonah felt the blood surging in his head, resentment in his heart. *If this is real repentance,* he thought, *why didn't it happen in Israel? Why aren't Israelites repenting at the preaching of the prophets?*

Fortunately, he had found an escape route and a hiding

place beneath the stairs of the palace. When he was finally alone, he hugged his knees in anguish. *I knew this would happen! What's going to become of me? If God doesn't destroy this city, my prophecy will not be fulfilled. What will people think of me?*

Fury churned within him and he could hold it in no longer. "O Lord, is this not what I said when I was still at home? That's why I was so quick to flee to Tarshish. I knew that you are a gracious and compassionate God, slow to anger, and abounding in love, a God who relents from sending calamity."

Anger and frustration consumed him. "Now, O Lord, take away my life, for it is better for me to die than to live." *Strike me dead,* he thought bitterly.

Instead, God answered him. "Have you any right to be angry?"

Jonah did not answer, and God did not speak again.

All night long Jonah was restless, fretful and fuming; but in the morning his hope was renewed, for an unnatural quiet hung over the city. *Perhaps they aren't repenting after all,* he thought. *Perhaps God will yet destroy Nineveh.*

Encouraged, Jonah gathered up his things. *I'd better get out of here,* he decided, and stealing down back streets, he hurried through the east gate to get outside the city. Going a safe distance up a hill that overlooked the river, he began breaking boughs to make a shelter from the sun. In forty days he would know the outcome.

Waiting was difficult. The nights were cold and the days hot. Bored with the view—he had counted the avenue of trees alongside the river a thousand times, the trees alternately tall and short; he had watched the river traffic until his eyes blurred—men riding astride inflated skins, poling peculiar round boats, casting nets. Nothing relieved the endless days, the scorching heat of the sun. Jonah scarcely ate, he was so disturbed.

God sees their works, he fumed, *that they're turning from their evil way.* Jonah fanned himself, drank more water, poured some on his head. *He'll forgive them,* he fretted, *judgment won't fall. Oh, why did this have to happen to me? At home they'll laugh me to scorn, say my prophecies don't come true.* Then he stormed out, "I don't care if Nineveh does repent, this city should be destroyed!"

No one heard him, and he lay down, sweltering under the sun.

One night a fast-growing plant began climbing up the boughs of Jonah's little booth. The broad leaves provided shade that brought blessed relief, and Jonah enjoyed the comfort it gave.

No sooner did he become accustomed to the pleasure of the plant, however, than a black caterpillar began rapidly eating its stems, leaves, and fruit. By morning the plant was withered and provided no shade at all. Worse still, a hot, dry wind from the desert was blowing vehemently. With the sun beating down on Jonah's head and the wind blasting him, he fainted dead away.

When he came to Jonah lay moaning. "It would be better for me to die than to live."

"Do you have a right to be angry about the vine?" God asked.

"I do," he answered, as obstinate as ever. "I am angry enough to die."

"You have been concerned about this vine, though you did not tend it or make it grow. It sprang up overnight and died overnight. But Nineveh has more than a hundred and twenty thousand people who cannot tell their right hand from their left, and many cattle as well. Should I not be concerned about that great city?" the Lord asked.

The question hung in the air, answering itself.

5

Daniel

NOW I, NEBUCHADNEZZAR, PRAISE AND EXALT AND GLO-
RIFY THE KING OF HEAVEN, BECAUSE EVERYTHING HE
DOES IS RIGHT AND ALL HIS WAYS ARE JUST.

Scripture Reference: Daniel 1–6

During the long journey from Jerusalem the Hebrew youths heard nothing but boasting from their captors. "We're rebuilding the greatest city in the world," they were told. "Grander than Nineveh, Thebes, or your miserable Jerusalem. You'll see walls—double walls, three hundred feet high and wide enough for four chariots to roll abreast on top of them; towers four hundred and twenty feet high—"

Daniel wasn't interested in Babylonian grandeur. His heart grew heavier as each passing mile took him farther and farther away from his home, his family, his friends. On the long weary journey they had passed Damascus, Tadmor, Mari, and Accad. To Daniel Babylon would be only another heathen city.

Three boys his own age—Hananiah, Mishael and Azariah—were in the wagon with him, but Daniel knew them only as fellow scholars from Jerusalem. At fifteen they were being taken away from everything they held dear for an unknown future, and Daniel purposed in his heart that whatever he faced he would honor the covenant and the God of the covenant.

In the cart ahead of them were the treasures from King Solomon's Temple taken by Nebuchadnezzar as tribute from Jehoiakim, king of Judah. Only a dirty linen cloth covered a golden lampstand propped against a crate of gold pitchers, plates, lamp snuffers, censers—all vessels consecrated to God. Thick yellow dust churned up by the wheels settled over the plunder piled on the cart and on the heavily armed guards walking alongside.

"Babylon's streets run straight this way and that," the guard in charge of them was explaining. "At right angles to one another, each street ends in a gate, each gate dedicated to a god—" On and on he talked. Seeing the boys' inattention, he warned them: "You must learn your way around, you know—learn our customs, or you will never be accepted in the Magi." Seeing the boys were not intimidated, he sought again to impress them. "We're rebuilding the Procession Way that leads from the Ishtar Gate south into the city. You'll see for yourselves what a grand reception we'll get, we the victors at Carchemish—flags flying, bands playing, bells ringing! Nebuchadnezzar left this place the crown prince, now he returns King and conqueror of the west. We'll march rank and file through the city to the Temple of Marduk where King Nebuchadnezzar will lay these treasures before our god."

Daniel nudged Mishael and pointed to the setting sun. "It's time for the evening sacrifice." The four of them turned to face west and, as they were accustomed to do, prayed toward the Temple in Jerusalem. The guard watched quietly, and when they were done he rode alongside them in silence as if he were curious to know more about them. As day after day he observed their practice, he talked less and less about Babylon and became friendlier toward them.

The convoy was approaching Babylon from the north, a long straggly column of horsemen and camel drivers, ox carts, wagons, and foot soldiers plodding along in the heat and dirt of the caravan road. A grove of palm trees up ahead was the first sign of the city. When the shimmering towers of Babylon came into view—mirage-like projections against the sky— cheers went up. Halting the rag-tag column, commanders or-

dered everyone to bathe in the Euphrates and in the morning
to dress in parade gear and be ready to march by sunrise.

Daniel rose early the next morning and stood on the bank
of the Euphrates watching a wicker boat slowly making its
way upriver. Along this river Abraham had traveled, leaving
idolatrous Ur of the Chaldees for the Promised Land. *Ironic,*
Daniel thought, *that now, centuries later, his descendants are
being brought back as captives to the same idolatrous region.* It
grieved him in his heart that God's people had brought this on
themselves, and it troubled him that the innocent, the God-
fearing Israelites, must also go to Babylon. The reasons were
not clear to him, but he knew God and trusted him that this,
too, was not without purpose. His only fear lay in himself, that
he would succumb to the pressures ahead and in some way
betray the Lord. *I must trust God for steadfast courage,* he told
himself.

Officers were marshalling the company into rank and file;
and when they were ready to begin their triumphal march into
Babylon Daniel joined his friends riding in the ox cart. Far up
ahead were the heralds, their pennants emblazoned with em-
blems of the gods; charioteers came next; and following them
were cavalrymen, their prancing steeds bedecked with decora-
tions. Marching soldiers escorted the captives and wagons of
plunder. Somewhere in the miles-long column rode King Nebuchadnezzar, the supreme ruler of all Babylon, accompanied
by his queen, the Median princess Amytis.

Just outside the city the Hebrews rode past the brick works
where sun-dried bricks lay side by side in long rows. The place
was a beehive of activity—animals and men straining at loading and pulling sledges of bricks and asphalt. An enormous
kiln for baking bricks was at the center; a round furnace with
top and bottom openings like a giant oven.

Up ahead they could hear the noise and commotion welcoming the procession.

As their turn came to cross the moat and enter the great Ishtar Gate, the Hebrew youths gazed at the beautiful glazed brick covered with blue lapis lazuli tiles. Lions and dragons were prominent in all the designs—bold reliefs of lion heads and charging lions all across the walls. Lion jewelry adorned the necks of women together with half-moon gold pieces, strings of pearls and corals, and precious stones.

Thousands of people thronged the walls, the streets, rooftops, latticed windows—the noise was deafening. Horns, flutes, timbrels, zithers, harps, and bagpipes sounded hymns to the temples of the gods while spectators clapped their hands, cheered, and danced.

As the boys rode through the city they saw new construction going up everywhere—a temple on the other side of the Euphrates, the foundations laid for a ziggurat, terraces being built. At all the building sites were foreign workmen, captives deported from their homelands working as artisans or laborers.

Azariah was trying to be heard above the noise. "I remember my father telling me that Babylon was built on the site of the Tower of Babel. From the way these people are behaving, I'd say sinners still thrive here."

Everywhere they looked there was idolatry. Their ears and eyes were assaulted with obscenities, debauchery of every kind, and Daniel wondered if there were any worshipers of God in all of Babylon.

The Hebrews were not allowed to enter the Temple when the treasures from Jerusalem were offered to Nabu and Marduk, for only the king approached the gods. Waiting outside, their hearts heavy as lead, Daniel, Hananiah, Mishael, and Azariah were told that they would now be given names after the Babylonian gods Bel, Rach, Mesha, and Nego: Belteshazzar, Shadrach, Meshach, and Abednego. It made them sick at heart.

The celebration in the streets was still going strong when

the boys were taken to their quarters and told to prepare for the King's banquet. That night, as the four assembled with the wise men who would be their teachers, their eyes had never seen such quantities of food—whole pigs, fish, wild game, shellfish, luscious fruits, every kind of herb and condiment.

The officer in charge of them explained. "This food has been offered to the gods. Only the best is fit for the gods."

"They eat unclean meat," Shadrach remarked to his friends, "pork and shellfish. I'll not touch it."

The commander hosting the meal called for attention. Raising his glass, he proposed a toast to the god Belus. No sooner was the toast completed than another followed, and another.

"I'll not toast their gods," Meshach said.

"Nor I," the others agreed.

"We must resolve not to let the Babylonians break down our loyalty to God," Daniel warned. "If they can't do it one way, they'll do it another. No doubt they'll try to distract us from giving God the worship he deserves and try to get us to be totally occupied with ourselves."

"Why do they eat so much?" Abednego asked.

The officer overheard him and answered, "It's a tribute to our gods to eat a lot. In that way we are showing that his favor has made us prosperous. Rather nice, don't you think, for in pleasing the gods one pleases himself."

"Gluttony is a moral evil," Abednego said.

Daniel turned to the officer and asked permission not to defile himself with the king's food.

The man frowned. Clearly he favored the Hebrews above the other youths who were under the tutelage of the wise men, but he did not wish to risk the king's displeasure. "I'm afraid of my lord the king, who has assigned your food and drink. Why should he see you looking worse than the other young men your age? The king would then have my head because of you."

Daniel pleaded, "Please test your servants for ten days: Give us nothing but vegetables to eat and water to drink. Then compare our appearance with that of the young men who eat the royal food, and treat your servants in accordance with what you see."

The officer looked at him quizzically. Then he gave a guarded reply. "Ten days only," he warned.

Even by the second day Shadrach, Meshach, Abednego, and Daniel could see how much better they fared than the other students. The others were suffering hangovers from the wine and biliousness from gorging themselves and were in no condition to undertake the strenuous schedule of studies required of them. They could not comprehend how to plot the movement of heavenly bodies, and fell asleep while making astronomical observations. While the four Hebrews were learning how to analyze the qualities of metals and minerals, the others were struggling over the elementary fundamentals of the science. In the process of time God gave the four knowledge and understanding of all kinds of literature and learning. When the chief official presented them to King Nebuchadnezzar for examination they outshone their fellows. In every matter of wisdom and understanding the king found them to be ten times superior to all the magicians and enchanters in his kingdom.

The next year Nebuchadnezzar chose to put his Magi to a test. Having dreamed a troublesome dream which he thought had meaning, he called together his astrologers, magicians, enchanters, and sorcerers to find out what his dreams meant.

The Magi answered, "O king, live forever! Tell your servants the dream, and we will interpret it."

Nebuchadnezzar leaned forward, his flinty eyes boring down. "This is what I have firmly decided: If you do not tell me what my dream was and interpret it, I will have you cut in pieces and your houses turned into piles of rubble. But if you tell me the dream and explain it, you will receive from me gifts

and rewards and great honor. So tell me the dream and interpret it for me."

With that he leaned back and twirled the goblet of wine in
his hand, waiting for their answer. Only if they could recall his
dream would there be reason to believe their interpretation. If
they could not recall it they would not be the first men he had
flayed alive or hacked to death.

Nothing in the Magis' training, knowledge passed from
father to son, equipped them to do what the king asked. They
could calculate the rise and set of planets, the pattern of their
orbits; they could predict storms, earthquakes, comets, eclipses;
they could interpret omens, prophesy, divine by rods, interpret
dreams; but nothing they knew enabled them to tell him what
he had dreamed.

These servants, looking worried, again asked Nebuchadnezzar to tell them the dream, assuring him they would then
interpret it. The king would not budge and told them they
were stalling to gain time. "If you do not tell me the dream,
there is just one penalty for you. You have conspired to tell me
misleading and wicked things, hoping the situation will
change. So then, tell me the dream, and I will know that you
can interpret it for me."

The astrologers answered, "There is not a man on earth
who can do what the king asks! No king, however great and
mighty, has ever asked such a thing of any magician or enchanter or astrologer. What the king asks is too difficult. No
one can reveal it to the king except the gods, and they do not
live among men."

Furious, King Nebuchadnezzar ordered the execution of
all the Magi. The decree was written and a search was begun
to ferret out all the wise men in Babylon.

Arioch, the commander of the king's guard, came to the
quarters where the four Hebrew youths lived, and Daniel met
him at the door. Trying to keep calm, Daniel, with wisdom
and tact, asked him, "Why did the king issue such a harsh
decree?"

When Arioch explained the reason, Daniel asked for an audience with the king. Nebuchadnezzar received the youth; and when Daniel asked for time and promised to interpret the dream for Nebuchadnezzar, the king relented.

Daniel ran all the way back to the house. Breathlessly he spoke in a torrent of words, telling Shadrach, Meshach, and Abednego the situation. "It's urgent that we plead for mercy from the God of heaven concerning this mystery so that we won't be executed with the rest of the wise men of Babylon."

Going to the latticed window that faced west toward the Temple in Jerusalem, the four youths fell on their knees in earnest prayer.

During the night the mystery was revealed to Daniel in a vision. Overjoyed, he praised and thanked the God of heaven.

The next morning, Daniel found Arioch sharpening his sword. "You can put away your sword," he told him. "Take me to the king and I will interpret his dream for him."

As Daniel was led down the long hallway of the palace, the soles of his sandals made a slapping sound on the stone floor that echoed in the awesome silence. As he approached Nebuchadnezzar's throne the king eyed the slender boy contemptuously. The cruel eyes bore down on him. "Are you able to tell me what I saw in my dream and interpret it?"

Daniel took a deep breath and, looking Nebuchadnezzar in the eye, replied, "No wise man, enchanter, magician, or diviner can explain to the king the mystery he has asked about, but there is a God in heaven who reveals mysteries." Nebuchadnezzar lifted his chin and his heavy-lidded eyes looked down at Daniel imperiously. "He has shown King Nebuchadnezzar what will happen in days to come. Your dream and the visions that passed through your mind as you lay on your bed are these:

"As you were lying there, O king, your mind turned to things to come, and the revealer of mysteries showed you what is going to happen. As for me, this mystery has been revealed to me, not because I have greater wisdom than other living men, but so that you, O king, may know the interpretation and that you may understand what went through your mind.

"You looked, O king, and there before you stood a large statue—an enormous, dazzling statue, awesome in appearance. The head of the statue was made of pure gold, its chest and arms of silver, its belly and thighs of bronze, its legs of iron, its feet partly of iron and partly of baked clay. While you were watching a rock was cut out, but not by human hands. It struck the statue on its feet of iron and clay and smashed them. Then the iron, the clay, the bronze, the silver, and the gold were broken to pieces at the same time and became like chaff on a threshing floor in the summer. The wind swept them away without leaving a trace but the rock that struck the statue became a huge mountain and filled the whole earth."

Greatly pleased, Nebuchadnezzar smiled and nodded then leaned forward, eager to hear the rest.

Daniel paused, then proceeded with the interpretation. Nebuchadnezzar's kingdom was the "head of gold." After him would come an inferior kingdom, followed by a third kingdom that would rule the whole earth. Finally, a fourth kingdom would arise in the world, very strong and crushing all the others. "As the toes were partly iron and partly clay, so this kingdom will be partly strong and partly brittle," Daniel told him, "and the people will be a mixture and will not be united."

He paused again, studying the face of Nebuchadnezzar so intent upon his every word. Impatient, the king rapped his scepter on the floor. Daniel then explained the stone as the kingdom of God that will never be destroyed. "The great God has shown the king what will take place in the future. The dream is true and the interpretation is trustworthy."

Nebuchadnezzar rose trembling from his throne and ordered his servants, "Offer incense to him. Bring lavish gifts for this youth!" And, falling prostrate before Daniel, the king paid him honor. "Surely your God is the God of gods," he said, "and the Lord of kings and a revealer of mysteries, for you were able to reveal this mystery."

Daniel knew the king's admission did not mean any change in him. All the idolaters he knew acknowledged a Supreme God of gods, but submission to the Lord to the exclusion of all false gods was never intended.

Nebuchadnezzar promoted Daniel to the position of ruler over all of Babylon and placed him in charge of all the Magi. At Daniel's request the king appointed Shadrach, Meshach, and Abednego administrators over the province of Babylon while Daniel remained at the royal court.

The knowledge that his kingdom was superior to all human successors swelled Nebuchadnezzar's heart with pride. In the months that followed he decided to build an image to symbolize the grandeur of Babylon and her chief god, Marduk. Daniel, traveling away from the city, was not available to advise the king nor to be tested by Nebuchadnezzar's next decree.

A few miles southeast of the city Nebuchadnezzar commissioned the building of a statue of gold, an obelisk ninety feet high and nine feet wide. A pedestal was set up in the plain of Dura, and the image of gold erected on it. All the provincial dignitaries were summoned to the dedication of the image, and on the day they were assembled the herald cried, "This is what you are commanded to do, O peoples, nations and men of every language: As soon as you hear the sound of the horn, flute, zither, lyre, harp, pipes and all kinds of music, you must fall down and worship the image of gold that King Nebuchadnezzar has set up. Whoever does not fall down and worship will immediately be thrown into a blazing furnace."

The musicians began tuning their instruments, but soon the cacophony of sounds ceased and the band began playing a stirring, militant hymn. The assembly dropped to their knees, bowed to the ground, and worshiped the image, sending up a great babel of languages in praise of Marduk.

Later in the day astrologers came to Nebuchadnezzar with the news that there were some Jews, set over the affairs of state, who "pay no attention to you, O king. They neither serve your gods nor worship the image of gold you have set up."

Nebuchadnezzar's countenance turned dark with fury. "Bring them here!" he shouted.

When Shadrach, Meshach, and Abednego were brought before him, the king offered them another chance. "When you hear the music," he said, "if you are ready to fall down and worship the image I made, very good." Scowling down at them, he added, "But if you do not worship it, you will be thrown immediately into a blazing furnace. Then what god will be able to rescue you from my hand?"

As if they had already discussed and agreed upon what they would say, the young men did not hesitate to answer. "O Nebuchadnezzar, we do not need to defend ourselves before you in this matter. If we are thrown into the burning furnace, the God we serve is able to save us from it, and he will rescue us from your hand, O king. But even if he does not, we want you to know, O king, that we will not serve your gods or worship the image of gold you have set up."

Their impertinence infuriated him. In a maniacal frenzy Nebuchadnezzar shouted orders to the captain of the guard, who was quick to obey. Hurrying to the brick works he delivered the message to Nebuchadnezzar's mighty men who were standing alongside the furnace. They were gigantic, muscular men dressed in richly ornamented costumes. The captain told them, "Heat the furnace seven times hotter than usual." As strong as they were, their faces blanched at the order—for such heat would threaten their own lives. Reluctantly they obeyed, knowing that to do otherwise would mean a painful death by torture. Stacking the fuel high in the kiln, they withdrew a safe distance away and waited for the flames to take hold, quaking in fear for what was coming next.

The victims, Shadrach, Meshach, and Abednego, were brought to the brick works dressed in their ordinary clothes—

inner and upper tunics, with a cloak worn on top of them, turbans on their heads, and sandals on their feet. King Nebuchadnezzar, members of the Magi, priests, and other dignitaries watched the proceedings with relish, bloodthirsty for the execution.

When the heat rose to maximum intensity the captain ordered the three Jewish youths to be bound. The mighty men took their time performing the task, making the crowd impatient, shouting angry epithets. Soaking themselves in water and stalling as long as they dared, the men had no choice but finally to throw the Jews in the kiln, although it meant certain death for them as well. Taking the youths by the arms and legs, they rushed toward the bottom opening and heaved them into the inferno. The blast of billowing flames blistered the flesh of the screaming guards, set their clothes ablaze! Swallowing flames, they staggered a few steps and fell writhing on the ground. Even after they were dead, their burning flesh sizzled in the flames.

Nebuchadnezzar watched, unmoved. Staring straight into the fire belching flames and ash from the opening, he thought his eyes were playing tricks on him. Bodily forms passed before the entrance—as if the youths were walking about in there! Nebuchadnezzar was counting them when suddenly he leaped to his feet. "Weren't there three men that we tied up and threw into the fire?"

"Certainly, O king," an aide replied.

"Look!" he exclaimed, his finger shaking, "I see four men walking around in the fire, unbound and unharmed, and the fourth looks like a son of the gods!"

People crowded closer to see, astonished at the sight.

Wetting his lips, Nebuchadnezzar shouted, "Shadrach, Meshach, and Abednego, servants of the Most High God, come out! Come here!"

One by one the boys climbed out through the opening and,

stepping around the grotesque, charred bodies of the dead men, approached the king. All the assembled dignitaries crowded around them, examining their hair, their clothing. "Scorched?" one asked as he sniffed, then shook his head in answer.

"Not a hair singed!" someone exclaimed. "How can this be?"

"There's no smell of smoke on them!"

Nebuchadnezzar, pale from fright, his voice a coarse whisper, spoke, "Praise be to the God of Shadrach, Meshach and Abednego, who has sent his angel and rescued his servants! They trusted in him and defied the king's command and were willing to give up their lives rather than serve or worship any god except their own God."

A murmur went through the crowd. Nebuchadnezzar held up his scepter for silence. "Therefore I decree that the people of any nation or language who say anything against the God of Shadrach, Meshach, and Abednego be cut into pieces and their houses be turned into piles of rubble, for no other god can save in this way."

Then he promoted the three Hebrew youths.

Eight years after Daniel and his three friends were taken to Babylon, another group of captives was deported from Jerusalem, Ezekiel among them. They settled on the Chebar, a tributary of the Euphrates, three hundred miles above Babylon and not far from the fortress city of Carchemish. Daniel learned through diplomatic channels that Jeremiah, the prophet, was still in Jerusalem.

With the exile of more Jews the outlook for Jerusalem was increasingly dismal. Knowing Nebuchadnezzar, Daniel knew he would not stop until the beloved city was destroyed, its people killed or taken captive.

Looking out the window toward his homeland Daniel wondered how his fellow Jews would fare in idolatrous Babylon. At one time he had counted fifty-three temples in Babylon, fifty-five chapels of Marduk, three hundred chapels for earth gods, six hundred for heavenly gods, a hundred and eighty altars for Ishtar, the chief goddess, and a hundred and eighty altars for Nergal and Adad.

He thought about the women and girls he'd seen going to the shrine of Aphrodite. Only after a woman gave herself to consort with a stranger was she allowed to go home. Beautiful females were quickly taken and released, but sometimes two or three years passed before the unattractive women were able to do their service to the goddess and go home.

Daniel was himself a young man of twenty-three. So far God had enabled him and his friends to keep their resolve, but the enticements were always there—the orgiastic festivals at every turn, the freely flowing wine, easy prostitution. As he stood before the window Daniel earnestly prayed that the abominable practices of the Babylonians would never become acceptable to him or any of the Jewish captives.

Five years after Ezekiel came to the Chebar he predicted the overthrow of Jerusalem and the devastation of Judah. False prophets among the captives disputed his word, but Daniel knew Ezekiel was telling the truth. From reading Jeremiah's prophecy he also learned that Jewish captives would be in Babylon seventy years. Jeremiah told them to build houses and settle down, marry, multiply, and seek the peace and prosperity of the city of their exile. "Pray to the Lord for it," he said, "because if it prospers, you too will prosper."

Daniel obeyed the word of God by Jeremiah. As a statesman in the government he sought the peace and prosperity of Babylon, and prayed for it every day. Never was there genuine peace; for Nebuchadnezzar was constantly engaged in aggressive warfare, and the prosperity was at the cost of oppressive taxation, plunder, and tribute.

When Daniel learned that Nebuchadnezzar had launched

another siege of Jerusalem he considered it would be the last. When Jerusalem fell, stories coming out of the siege were of atrocities. The Babylonians spared neither child nor aged person—maiming, impaling, skinning alive, torturing those they killed, and with relentless fury pursuing famished fugitives. Edomites joined in the chase and hounded the Jews, tracking them to holes and caves. The dead were piled high, princes hanged by their hands, others buried alive in subterranean dungeons on the shores of the Dead Sea. The Temple smoldered in ashes.

Daniel was thirty-three when the end came. For the next thirteen years he would serve an absentee king, for Nebuchadnezzar spent those years besieging Tyre. When Tyre was finally taken and Nebuchadnezzar came home to Babylon, he found an older, wiser Daniel, a man of forty-six who had dealt with the contrary Magi, with difficult problems of state, and in it all resisted compromise with the heathen culture, remaining steadfast in his integrity and faith in God.

Even so, Daniel's name did not come to Nebuchadnezzar at once when, for a second time, he experienced terrifying visions. He called for his magicians but none could interpret the dreams for him. Then he called for Daniel in whom, he remembered, was "the spirit of the holy gods."

The dream concerned an enormous tree which gave food and shelter to beasts and birds. Then a "holy one" coming from heaven commanded that the tree be cut down and stripped. Its stump and roots, banded with iron and bronze, was to be left. "Let him be drenched with the dew of heaven, and let him live with the animals among the plants of the earth. Let his mind be changed from that of a man and let him be given the mind of an animal till seven times pass by for him."

For some time Daniel was perplexed and alarmed by what the king told him. Seeing this, Nebuchadnezzar tried to set his mind at ease. "Belteshazzar, do not let the dream or its meaning alarm you."

"If only the dream applied to your enemies," Daniel replied

sadly. "You are that tree! Your dominion extends to distant parts of the earth. You will be cut down like that tree. O king, this is the decree the Most High has issued against my lord the king: You will be driven away from people and will live with the wild animals; you will eat grass like cattle and be drenched with the dew of heaven."

The king's face seemed set in stone.

"Therefore, O king, be pleased to accept my advice: Renounce your sins by doing what is right and your wickedness by being kind to the oppressed. It may be that then your prosperity will continue."

Nebuchadnezzar shrugged his shoulders indifferently and held his glass for more wine. Sadly, Daniel withdrew. Without repentance there would be no clemency.

One year later the dream was fulfilled. As Nebuchadnezzar was walking on the roof of his palace in Babylon he thought upon the multitudes of captives doing his pleasure—goldsmiths, artists, builders; the plunder he had taken from countries far and near—gold, silver, ivory, horses, chariots. And as he looked out over the city he was overcome by the grandeur of all he beheld. "Is not this the great Babylon I have built as the royal residence, by my mighty power and for the glory of my majesty?"

While the words were still on his lips, a voice spoke from heaven. "Your royal authority has been taken from you. You will be driven away from people and will live with the wild animals; you will eat grass like cattle. Seven times will pass by for you until you acknowledge that the Most High is sovereign over the kingdoms of men and gives them to anyone he wishes."

Right away, it was apparent that Nebuchadnezzar had lost his mind. Stricken with the delusion that he was an animal, Nebuchadnezzar began snorting like a wild ox, making unnatural lowing sounds. Storming about he smashed crockery, broke furniture, threatened life and limb of anyone in his way. In desperation his servants turned him out in a field and watched in horror as he fell on hands and knees, grazing like a beast!

In the weeks and months that followed nothing could be done for Nebuchadnezzar. Unwilling to be tended, his nails grew long like claws, his hair thick and matted.

While Nebuchadnezzar was ill his son, Evil-Merodach, ruled in his stead; but when his father recovered a year later Nebuchadnezzar threw his son in prison.

Surprisingly well after his pasture diet, Nebuchadnezzar regained control of the kingdom and glorified the Most High who lives forever. Nebuchadnezzar told his nobles, "Now I, Nebuchadnezzar, praise and exalt the King of heaven, because everything he does is right and all his ways are just. And those who walk in pride he is able to humble."

Nebuchadnezzar continued his military campaigns and building operations until, after a brief illness, he died. He was followed by three weak kings, the last of them a man from Haran, Nabonidus. Unlike Nebuchadnezzar, who allowed considerable authority to the priesthood in making decisions about irrigation and agriculture, Nabonidus antagonized priests all over the empire by confiscating idols from temples and sending them to Babylon.

It had been nearly fifty years since Daniel had interpreted Nebuchadnezzar's dream of the image with the head of gold, but he was beginning to realize that the time had come for the next phase of the dream to be fulfilled. As he heard more and more about the exploits of the Medes, as he reviewed Isaiah's prophecy concerning Cyrus, the Mede, it became increasingly apparent that the kingdom of Babylon would soon be overrun. While the Medes and Persians were on the move, Nabonidus devoted ten years to the conquest of northern Arabia and made his headquarters in the oasis of Temna. He sought to unify

Babylon by making Haran's moon god, Sin, the chief god of
the state, and that turned the priests of Marduk against him.
They began to listen to the overtures of Cyrus. Engrossed in
his archaeological pursuits, Nabonidus appointed Belshazzar,
a descendant, to the kingship.

Unfortunately, Belshazzar felt secure in Babylon with his
standing army, the city's impregnable walls and moat, and
with food supplies for a twenty-year siege stored in the granaries. He maintained a continual round of feasting and celebrating of the gods. Each spring the New Year's festival saw all the
gods of the empire transported by ship and wagon from the
provinces to the city, where they stood before the statue of
Marduk in the great hall of his temple. Together the gods were
trusted to determine each man's fortune for the coming year.

Belshazzar tried always to outdo himself with each feast he
gave. No orgy was too wild, no expense too much to satiate
his lusts. On one such occasion the tables were spread for a
thousand guests and vats of wine were at their disposal. Belshazzar, robed in splendor, sat on the throne on a raised platform, drinking before his nobles and their women. Knowing
the awesome regard some of his subjects had for the God of the
Jews, he startled them by demanding that the gold and silver
goblets from the Jews' Temple in Jerusalem be brought for
their use.

The vessels were distributed among the guests, and servants filled them with wine. Belshazzar raised his goblet and
toasted the gods of gold and silver, of bronze, iron, wood, and
stone! Raising the cup to his lips he drained the last drop. Just
as he did he heard a gasp in the hushed crowd. His eyes
followed the crowd's to the right wall of the banquet hall. The
fingers of a human hand, right above the lampstand, were
writing on the wall! Color drained from the king's face as he
watched.

When the writing was finished and the hand removed,
Belshazzar kept staring, transfixed. Finally he found his voice
and feebly called for the Magi. "Whoever reads this writing

and tells me what it means will be clothed in purple and have a gold chain placed around his neck, and he will be made the third highest ruler in the kingdom."

The wise men were summoned and brought running to the room. Gazing open-mouthed at the words scrawled on the wall, they were totally mystified. Terror rising in him, Belshazzar was beside himself.

Hearing the disturbances the Queen Mother, Nitocris, moving slowly and leaning on a cane, hobbled into the hall. Seeing the handwriting, the Magi stricken dumb, she perceived the problem and proceeded to tell Belshazzar what she knew. "O king, live forever! Don't look so pale! There is a man in your kingdom who has the spirit of the holy gods in him." She shuffled closer to Belshazzar, the better to see him, and peering at him said, "This man whom Nebuchadnezzar called Belteshazzar was found to have a keen mind and knowledge and understanding, and also the ability to interpret dreams, explain riddles, and solve difficult problems. Call for Daniel, and he will tell you what the writing means."

So Daniel was called. The king repeated his offer of gifts and honor, but Daniel shook his head. He felt weary and old, sad at the prospects for the young king before him. In a voice that was no longer strong Daniel answered, "You may keep your gifts for yourself and give your rewards to someone else. Nevertheless, I will read the writing for the king and tell him what it means."

Daniel waited, feeling the gravity of his words. "O king, the Most High God gave your father Nebuchadnezzar sovereignty and greatness and glory and splendor. Because of the high position he gave him, all the peoples and nations and men of every language dreaded and feared him. Those the king wanted to put to death, he put to death; those he wanted to spare, he spared; those he wanted to promote, he promoted; and those he wanted to humble, he humbled. But when his heart became arrogant and hardened with pride he was deposed from his royal throne and stripped of glory. He was driven away from people and given the mind of an animal; he lived with wild donkeys and ate grass like cattle; and his body was drenched with the dew of heaven, until he acknowledged that the Most High God is sovereign over the kingdoms of men and sets over them anyone he wishes.

"But you his son, O Belshazzar, have not humbled yourself, though you knew all this." He paused, letting the words take full effect. "Instead, you have set yourself up against the Lord of heaven. You had the goblets from his temple brought to you, and you and your nobles, your wives and your concubines drank wine from them. You praised the gods of silver and gold, of bronze, iron, wood and stone, which cannot see or hear or understand. But you did not honor the God who holds in his hand your life and all your ways. Therefore he sent the hand that wrote the inscription."

So agitated his knees were knocking, Belshazzar looked as if he might faint.

Daniel studied the inscription and read it aloud. *"Mene, mene, tekel, parsin."* Overcome with the significance of what he was about to say, Daniel was quiet for a moment. During all the years he had served in Babylon, he had known that this day would come, yet he grieved that only judgment was left for Babylon. His sadness was tempered by the relief of knowing the Jews would soon be allowed to return to Jerusalem.

Addressing the king, Daniel told him, *"Mene* means God has numbered the days of your reign and brought it to an end."

Belshazzar stared back at him, horrified.

"Tekel means you have been weighed on the scales and found wanting. *Peres* means your kingdom is divided and given to the Medes and Persians."

Belshazzar looked frozen with fear. Hoping for another word, his eyes were pleading. But no further word was given.

In a little while Belshazzar cleared his throat and, speaking softly, he told his servants to clothe Daniel in purple with a gold chain around his neck. Then, lifting his scepter, he proclaimed him the third ruler in the kingdom under Nabonidus and himself.

Later that night Daniel watched from the window as the army of Medes and Persians streamed through the gates of the city. In some manner the invaders had succeeded in draining the moat by diverting the water of the Euphrates. The takeover was relatively peaceful. Priests and people were in the streets welcoming the invaders. Only the screams from the palace evidenced bloodshed. Daniel turned away from the window. Soon they would be bringing the remains of Belshazzar out of the palace.

With the advent of the new regime Daniel had no position in the government. But when Darius organized the kingdom he appointed one hundred and twenty satraps with three administrators supervising them, one of whom was Daniel.

Daniel understood the satraps' dissatisfaction with him. Because he held them to the strictest of standards, their corrupt practices were curtailed and they suffered losses of graft. Daniel's administration so pleased Darius that he proposed making him head over the entire kingdom. Other administrators and satraps immediately set about to thwart the appointment. Meeting clandestinely, they sought some chink in Daniel's armor, some negligence in his performance, some irregularity, some incompetence. Finding none, they agreed, "We will never find any basis for charges against this man Daniel unless it has something to do with the law of his God."

They were all thinking about Daniel's recent fast when for three weeks he wore sackcloth and ashes and prayed continually. The more they thought about it, the more they saw the possibilities. Under ordinary conditions, Daniel was in the habit of praying three times a day before a western window facing Jerusalem where the Temple had stood. Nothing deterred him—not business, nor weather, nor ill health. They saw his intransigence in the matter as something making him vulnerable for entrapment. For some time the satraps considered different plans and finally agreed upon one.

With the conspiracy in mind, a delegation went to Darius and suggested that he impress his subjects with his authority as the representative of deity, by requiring that all requests be made to him and that prayer to any god be outlawed for thirty days.

"And the penalty for noncompliance?" he asked.

They had thought of that as well. "The lions' den," they answered.

A pleased look came over Darius's face. Flattered by the suggestion, consent was granted and the law was written.

Daniel heard about the decree as he was supervising the packing of the Temple treasures to be taken back to Jerusalem. The decree of Cyrus permitting the Jews to return to the homeland was a source of great joy to Daniel even though, at his age, he could not return with them.

Then Daniel's friends came, tears in their eyes, to tell him about the decree.

Not until all the crates were packed did Daniel leave the palace or give himself time to consider the consequences of the decree. On the way home he stopped to rest by a fountain in one of the public squares where there was a little garden. The news was not surprising nor did he doubt for a moment who was behind it. He was well aware of the opposition and the cunning of the underlings. They would stop at nothing to get rid of him. Still the imminence of the danger took some getting used to.

An old man Daniel's age was sitting by the fountain, all bent over, leaning on a cane. The man's cloudy eyes were so dim he seemed to be asleep and unaware that anyone was near by. Daniel often saw him there, but when he tried to talk with him the man only mumbled. *His brain is dying*, Daniel thought. *So many men in their eighties are children in their heads.*

Daniel rubbed his knee. *Better to have joints that creak than lose one's senses,* he told himself.

The breeze blowing in from the river was refreshing and the fragrance of the blossoms in the garden scented the air. Loving life as he did, Daniel did not seek to die. *And yet,* he thought, *since I've lived to see the exile ended, and God has given me his message to enable our people to live through the difficult times ahead, perhaps my work is over.* He tried not to think about the horrors of the lions' den.

Noting the slant of the sun he saw that it was time to go, and got up.

When Daniel reached his home he took down the prayer shawl just inside the door, draped it over his head, and climbed the stairs. The latticed window facing the setting sun cast a checked shadow on the floor. Opening the lattice Daniel kneeled down and began praying aloud.

Spies from the delegation were hiding beneath the window and saw Daniel at the window facing west. Hearing his words as he prayed, they were delighted; but until they had observed him several times in prayer and had several witnesses to the fact, they did not inform the king.

When the evidence was indisputable the accusers, with profound politeness, asked Darius, "Did you not publish a decree that during the next thirty days anyone who prays to any god or man except to you, O king, would be thrown into the lions' den?"

Darius answered, "The decree stands—in accordance with the laws of the Medes and Persians, which cannot be annulled."

The men looked at each other with amused satisfaction. "Daniel, who is one of the exiles from Judah, pays no attention to you, O king, or to the decree you put in writing. He still prays three times a day."

Darius looked aghast. Daniel was his favorite! The trap was snapped shut and held him fast, for the law of the Medes and the Persians could not be changed. Darius immediately set about to seek every possible means to spring that trap.

Anxiously the delegation waited until sundown. Then, nervously, they approached Darius again. "Remember, O king, that according to the law of the Medes and Persians no decree or edict that the king issues can be changed."

Darius had exhausted every recourse trying to spare Daniel, but to no avail. Smarting under the requirements of the law, he squared his jaw and proceeded to carry out its demands.

When the day of execution arrived, Daniel was brought to the lions' den, his weeping friends following. The king met him there, and to give the friends time to bid their farewells Darius stood watching the lions pacing back and forth in the cage. It was a blistering hot day, and the animals had not been fed as the custom was when there was to be an execution. They roared from hunger, their great yellow fangs showing.

When the farewells were over Darius, visibly disturbed, gave Daniel a parting word, "May your God, whom you serve continually, rescue you!"

The cage had two openings, one at the top and one on the side. The top opening was too far above the head of a man for a prisoner to escape that way, and the side opening would be sealed. Guards rolled a stone over the side opening and stretched a cord across the stone, fastening it on either side. Then a lump of clay was pressed against each end of the cord and the king's signet ring, as well as the rings of his nobles, were impressed on the clay. In that way no one would dare release the lions or Daniel, for whoever broke the governmental seals would be put to death.

The entrance sealed, Darius reluctantly gave the order to the guards. Moving at Daniel's own feeble pace they respectfully assisted him up the ladder that led to the trap door on top of the cage. There they paused to give him a moment to prepare himself. Daniel spoke kindly to them, told them he was ready. One of them opened the door and another gave Daniel a slight push, toppling him into the den.

The fall stunned Daniel and he lay on the floor dazed. As he was coming to a lion was standing over him, sniffing about his face. Daniel lay still, expecting the lion to open its jaws and clamp down on his head.

Instead, the lion lost interest and moved off of him!

In the intense heat the animals were restless, pacing all around Daniel, their great manes like collars, their big paws with claws retracted, observing him ominously. A lean and hungry lion, its flanks sunken, its sides ribbed, nuzzled him, bared its teeth, then turned away. One of the females, lapping water from a trough, stopped and stared at him hungrily, her tail going back and forth. Then she yawned and, ambling over to her half-grown cub, laid down. As Daniel lay on the floor he became aware of the presence of a messenger from God in the den! The other animals began circling him, seeking space—a bit of shade—to lie down in. One by one the tawny beasts stretched out on the floor and lay panting, their tongues lolling. From time to time they yawned, opening wide their great jaws, and settled down to sleep. In the unbearable heat they lay listless, barely lifting their tails to ward off flies.

Only then did Daniel fully realize that he was in no danger; God was indeed going to spare his life. Tired as he was, he made himself as comfortable as he could and tried to rest.

In the morning, when the first streaks of light reached the den, Daniel heard Darius calling him. "Daniel, servant of the living God, has your God, whom you serve continually, been able to rescue you from the lions?"

Daniel smiled and answered the king. "O king, live forever! My God sent his angel, and he shut the mouths of the lions. They have not hurt me, because I was found innocent in his sight. Nor have I ever done any wrong before you, O king."

He heard the king's excited voice barking orders to his men, then he heard the stone scraping as it was being rolled away. And the next minute Daniel, stooping to make his exit, crawled through the opening. Curious to see if he was hurt in any way, officers examined him and could not find a scratch on him. Daniel's friends rushed upon him, hugging, kissing, weeping for joy.

The satrap delegation was standing nearby, wide-eyed and shaking from head to toe. King Darius ordered them and their families arrested. Daniel had no desire to witness their fate and left the scene. Later he heard that the lions made quick work of them.

That same day Darius made a decree. In it he commanded fear and reverence for the God of Daniel.

> For he is the living God
>   and he endures forever;
> his kingdom will not be destroyed,
>   his dominion will never end.
> He rescues and he saves;
>   he performs signs and wonders
>   in the heavens and on the earth.
> He has rescued Daniel
>   from the power of the lions.

From the distant past, Daniel remembered similar words spoken by Nebuchadnezzar. "I'll wait and see," he said. "Perhaps—"

Part II

New Testament Experiences

6

Mary

BUT MARY TREASURED UP ALL THESE THINGS AND POND-
ERED THEM IN HER HEART.

Scripture Reference: Isaiah 7:14; Luke 1:1–56; Matthew 1:18–25

The stone floor of the synagogue was cold beneath her feet but Mary scarcely noticed, straining as she was to hear the man who was praying. She knew by heart all the prayers of the *Shemoneh 'Esreh*—three in praise of God, thirteen petitions, and three thanksgivings. Today, only the first and last three prayers would be recited, with a single prayer substituted for the thirteen omitted. The voice droned on, barely audible in the far reaches of the women's section. Bored, the women chatted with one another and gave no heed to what was being spoken.

Mary tried hard to keep her mind from wandering although it was difficult with Joseph sitting on the other side in clear view. She dare not cast a sidelong glance at him lest the women chide her. Nathan, Joseph's friend, was faithful in going back and forth between them, and plied Mary with credits in Joseph's favor. "Not everyone can trace his ancestry," Nathan told her, "but Joseph's ancestry is carefully preserved because he is of the house of David."

What mattered most to Mary was that Joseph was a fair man, and a hard-working, skilled carpenter. He would not undertake marriage if he was not able to support a wife and family.

Mary remembered the evening a year before, when Joseph's father and Nathan had come to speak with her father—

first with a promise of marriage, later to make the betrothal covenant. There were gifts of garments and a garnet necklace for her. Both families gathered in the courtyard of her father's home with witnesses to attest the covenant. Red of face, Joseph placed a gold ring on her finger saying, "See by this ring you are set apart for me, according to the law of Moses and of Israel."

With appropriate modesty her eyes met his, and in that one swift glance the earnestness in his young face made her feel glad inside.

Even so Mary, young as she was, had misgivings that she may not measure up as a wife among the more mature women of Nazareth. "They bake, they sew," she fretted, "they take care of children, work in the vineyards, the olive groves—" She sighed. "Perhaps he'll change his mind."

"Don't worry," Nathan told her, "only a breach of the betrothal vows can break the covenant. A breach of the vows would be considered adultery, which never could happen with you. But even if it did, Mary, the betrothal could be dissolved only by divorce. Joseph loves you, silly girl. And, unless I am deceived, you love him." He cocked his eye at her questioningly but, seeing no response, continued. "Think of it this way, Mary—in a few months you'll be a married woman with your very own home with no one to look after but Joseph and his old father, Jacob."

The prospect filled her with anticipation and her imagination ran away with her. When the prayer ended Mary caught herself daydreaming and, feeling sorry, turned her attention back to the service.

The ruler of the synagogue asked a young man to read from Moses. He was the leather-worker's son, the one who wished to become a scribe. Blond and fair skinned, he mounted the raised platform nervously. With a grave expression on his face he unrolled the scroll for the reading of the day; but when he could not find the place amused women tittered behind the lattice that shielded them from view. The ruler came to the boy's aid. Flustered, his prayer shawl slipping down the back

of his head, the youth began. In an unsteady voice he read from
Deuteronomy in Hebrew and, verse by verse, translated it into
Aramaic.

Mary listened carefully, recording the words in memory
for she could scarcely read. Unlike Jewish boys, who attended
synagogue school, she knew only what her mother had taught
her at home. All schooling was by rote, and Mary's mind was
trained to memorize quickly and easily. Turning the phrases
over and over in her head, as with her sister Salome, they
became the warp and woof of her life.

Even so, she envied the elders sitting on the front row who
not only could read but spent most of their time studying the
Torah. She wondered if other women yearned as she did for
more knowledge of the scriptures.

No more than fifty people attended Sabbath services, for
Nazareth was a small village and not all its villagers were
Jewish. Of those fifty, seventeen were women. Three Greeks
attended irregularly and considered themselves to be God-
fearers but not proselytes, for they were not circumcised.

After the Deuteronomy passage there followed the reading
from the prophets. Clumsily the young man struggled with the
scroll until he found Daniel. As he read Mary knew the sermon
would raise lively debate among the men.

When the reading of scripture was finished an elder, chosen by the ruler, took the seat before the chest containing the
scrolls and delivered the sermon. With keen logic he sought to
convince the congregation that Daniel's seventy weeks were
about to run their course. The other elders interrupted noisily,
registering their disagreements, while one old man slept, his
chin on his chest and snoring loudly. Farmers and the like, too
intimidated by the leaders to raise their voices, listened eagerly,
wanting most of all to believe the Messiah would soon come.

The sermon ended but the heated discussion was only mo-
mentarily suspended. In the absence of a priest a prayer substituted for the benediction followed by the congregation's
"Amen." Then the debate resumed noisier than before.

Mary did not linger to talk with the women nor to wait for

Salome, who would stay and chat, but hurried outside to be well on her way home before the worshipers disbanded. Neither did she want Nathan to come chasing after her. She had given him a message for Joseph which he would deliver after the service, and it would be unseemly to appear to be waiting for an answer so soon.

A short distance from the synagogue were the precipitous cliffs, some of them as high as fifty feet, and walking along the edge Mary enjoyed the view in the early April night. Moonlight streaming down over Mount Tabor cast a luminous mantle of pearl, softening the harsh ridges, molding the shapes of stones.

Winding between Mount Tabor and the hills of Nazareth was the ancient Great Road West, or the Way of the Sea, a caravan route from the distant East to the distant West. Past the Hill of Precipitation, the steep road from Jerusalem climbed up to enter Nazareth, and to the northeast a road dropped down to the Sea of Galilee by way of Cana. All her life Mary had observed the heavily laden travelers, wondering what exotic wares they carried, and watched Roman soldiers in their scarlet capes going to and from their military posts.

As she took the road descending into town Mary could see most of the village spread out below. Nazareth, its white limestone houses nestled in a basin surrounded by a low-lying escarpment, was sometimes ridiculed for its bad manners and morals. Its reputation aside, Nazareth in moonlight was as fair a place as one could seek. Mary could think of no other place as home. To her the houses were beautifully situated among fig trees, olive groves, and the graceful, slender cypress, unequaled even in Capernaum. Down about the village well were gardens, surrounded by prickly-pear hedges, where vegetation thrived.

The dusty road was rutted from the wheels of wagons, and animal droppings made her cautious as she walked. In her heart she felt a certain joy which gave her the urge to skip along the road but, it being the Sabbath, she restrained herself. Passing between two houses, one with a dovecote on the roof, she listened for the contented cooing sounds of birds roosting there. But as she drew alongside something startled the doves; all at once they fluttered from their nests and, flocking into the air, flew up and away.

Surprised and somewhat puzzled, Mary paused at the gate of the second house. Suddenly, a man appeared out of nowhere.

"Greetings," he said, "you who are highly favored! The Lord is with you."

Startled, Mary did not know what to think. His words so troubled her she could not speak.

"Do not be afraid, Mary, you have found favor with God." He moved a step closer, laid his hand on the gate.

Her heart thumping in her chest, Mary realized he was not an ordinary man. *He's an angel of God!*

"You will be with child and give birth to a son . . ."

The words baffled her. *With child? Give birth?*

"You are to give him the name Jesus. He will be great and will be called the Son of the Most High."

Whatever does he mean? she wondered, her heart pounding.

"The Lord God will give him the throne of his father David, and he will reign over the house of Jacob forever; his kingdom will never end."

Her lips dry, her heart palpitating wildly, Mary's mind was racing. *I'm not married. How—* Totally confused, she blurted out, "How will this be since I am a virgin?"

The angel glanced up at the flock of doves returning, then replied, "The Holy Spirit will come upon you, and the power of the Most High will overshadow you."

Stunned, she was barely aware of the doves swirling overhead, their wings beating, seeking out their nests.

"So the holy one to be born will be called the Son of God," he told her, his voice strong and reassuring.

Astonished as she was, a certain joy began to take hold of her. Then the angel added this: "Even Elizabeth your relative is going to have a child in her old age, and she who was said to be barren is in her sixth month." He paused, looking down at her kindly. "For nothing is impossible with God."

Mary's hands were cold, her body trembling. Returning the man's kindly gaze she said as simply as she knew how, "I am the Lord's servant. May it be to me as you have said."

Acknowledging her submissiveness with a nod of his head, and while she was still looking at him, the angel disappeared.

Mary felt profoundly shaken and it was some time before, unconsciously, she began to move along. Walking ever so slowly, her thoughts raced.

No one must know of this, she resolved. *Not even Salome. Certainly no one would believe— He will be called* the Son of God! . . . *What would father think. What if— I dare not imagine what the neighbors in Nazareth will say if they get wind of this.*

Hearing voices in the distance, Mary quickened her step lest the returning worshipers overtake her.

That night, lying on the pallet beside her sister, Mary waited until steady breathing assured her that Salome was sleeping. Then, sitting up, she let go the worries that would disturb her and, reviewing what the angel had told her, became excited. *"Call him Jesus, Son of the Most High—" Such words are beyond me! "Give him the throne of his father David—" This child, this baby will sit on David's throne? Fulfill the covenant . . . bring to pass God's promise to David! Oh, can it be that I . . . that this child to be born to me is to be a* king . . . *a king over a kingdom that will* never end!

In her excitement she had forgotten the news about Elizabeth, and remembering that she, too, was being favored, Mary was beside herself with joy. Elizabeth's miracle called to mind Hannah who had also been barren, although not as old as

Elizabeth, and the great joy Hannah expressed when God gave her a son. Mary had found it easy to learn Hannah's hymn of praise and, being somewhat poetically gifted herself, Mary began making up in her mind her own hymn of joy using scriptural phrases and words of her own.

Not once did she close her eyes. All night long her mind went back and forth from the ecstatic to the sublime as she pondered what the message meant and considered what practical action to take.

As day began to dawn Mary had made up her mind; but because it was the Sabbath she waited until the first day of the week to carry out her plan. The angel's mention of Elizabeth seemed to be a directive, the proper course to pursue. Packing a few garments, some food and water, she prepared for the journey to visit Elizabeth. Without telling her father or Salome the reason she left on horseback, traveling in the company of a family going to Emmaus.

Mary was anxious to reach Elizabeth, for if anyone would understand her situation Elizabeth would. For a woman who was past the age of child-bearing, one who had always been sterile, to have a child was a miracle. The angel's words declared it: *For nothing is impossible with God.*

Elizabeth's case reminded Mary of barren Sarah, Abraham's wife, who was more than ninety years old when she bore the son from whom all Jews on the face of the earth descended. *Surely he is the God of the impossible*, Mary thought, . . . *and there were also the barren wives of Isaac and Jacob. Elizabeth's miracle is not the first of its kind.*

As the horse beneath her kept to his steady gait, Mary considered the reproach Elizabeth had suffered in not being able to bear a son—so shameful was her plight, rabbis had told her husband a separation was their religious duty. Mary thought about how often they must have cried out to God, weeping. How many sleepless nights did they walk the floor before they gave up hope thinking their prayer was denied.

Now, Mary realized, *all that heartache is past—Elizabeth will cradle a son in her arms!* Joy welled up in Mary's soul and words of praise flowed easily. The lyrical rhythm lent itself to a melody, and Mary hummed the song as she rode on ahead of the others.

Camping that night, Mary sat up long after the family had bedded down in a cave. Watching the embers of the campfire dying, the Holy Spirit seemed to consume her, giving her such joy she could not contain herself. Looking up at the stars she whispered her praise to the Almighty God, her cheeks wet with tears of gratitude.

On the third day the traveling companions reached Emmaus. From there it was only a short ride to the village where Elizabeth lived.

Zachariah was standing in front of the house when Mary rode up the dusty street, and he greeted her with a wave of his hand. Mary dismounted and spoke to him, but he didn't reply. She handed him the reins, puzzled by his silence.

As she entered the house she called out, "Peace!" and Elizabeth, turning around, exclaimed, "Blessed are you among women, and blessed is the child you will bear!" Her wrinkled face was radiant!

The women reached out their arms to each other. As they were embracing Elizabeth drew back and asked, "But why am I so favored, that the mother of my Lord should come to me?" Clutching Mary's hand, she led her to the table. "As soon as the sound of your greeting reached my ears, the baby in my womb leaped for joy."

Astonished that Elizabeth already knew of her condition, Mary was eager to hear more. The spirit of prophecy was upon the older woman in a way Mary had never known before.

Elizabeth's eyes brimmed with tears. "Blessed is she who has believed that what the Lord has said to her will be accomplished!"

Mary bowed her head. From somewhere deep inside her, the Holy Spirit was prompting words of praise—scripture phrases and her own words knitting together in Hebrew rhythms such as she had heard all her life. In a voice so low she scarcely heard it herself, the words poured forth.

> My soul praises the Lord
>   and my spirit rejoices in God my Savior,
> for he has been mindful
>   of the humble state of his servant.

Elizabeth reached for her hand and held it in both her own. Hannah's words of praise came to mind, and for one brief moment Mary felt joined to all women blessed of God in special ways.

> From now on all generations will call me blessed,
> for the Mighy One has done great things for me—
> holy is his name.

In the silence that followed, she heard nothing but the beating of her own heart. The awesome fullness of God exhilarated her, and the words flowed freely—

> His mercy extends to those who fear him,
>   from generation to generation.
> He has performed mighty deeds with his arm;
>   he has scattered those who are proud
>   in their inmost thoughts.

Mary closed her eyes. Not a Babylonian or Persian prince had stood long against the Lord, nor would the Romans prevail. The King was coming! Little Israel, heir of the promises made to Abraham, would be exalted, favored by God.

He has brought down rulers from their thrones
    but has lifted up the humble.
He has filled the hungry with good things
    but has sent the rich away empty.
He has helped his servant Israel,
    remembering to be merciful
to Abraham and his descendants forever,
    even as he said to our fathers.

When the hymn ended the two women sat quietly worshiping God, overwhelmed by the mystery of what was taking place.

After taking care of the horse Zachariah came inside and joined Mary and Elizabeth at the table. Unable to speak, Elizabeth spoke for him, explaining to Mary about Gabriel's visit to Zachariah.

For the next three months Mary remained with Elizabeth and Zachariah, helping with the chores, praying, talking. But when it was time for Elizabeth's son to be born Mary packed her things and bid them farewell. It was time to tell Joseph.

Back in Nazareth Mary sent word to Nathan that she must see Joseph, that it was urgent. That evening Joseph met her at the village well. Taking him aside from the other women, Mary had him sit down behind the hedge of the little garden there.

"I've missed you, Mary. You left without saying good-bye."

She pressed a finger to his lips. "You'll understand when I tell you. Do you remember the last time you saw me in the synagogue? It happened that night as I was coming home."

"What happened?"

She drew a deep breath. "This will be difficult, Joseph
. . . please, it's not for us to understand . . . only believe."

"Believe what, Mary?"

And then she told him.

The look on his face was answer enough. He did not believe her. "It's been three months?" he asked, his eyes averted.

She nodded. When she touched his arm hoping to explain,
he drew away from her. "I must think about this," he said
softly, and the pain in his eyes was unbearable to see. "As soon
as I've made a decision, I'll let you know."

As he walked away from her, devastated, Mary fought back
the tears.

When Joseph was out of sight she turned back to the chore
of drawing water. Relieved that the other women had left the
well and were on their way home, Mary lowered the bucket,
preoccupied as she was with the painful difficulties ahead. *Well,*
she said to herself, *if it must be this way there is nothing I can
do. Unless God intends otherwise, Joseph will divorce me.* Tears
stung her eyes. *Perhaps he will spare me a public denunciation
. . . yet he is a just man . . . thinking ill of me, he may consider
that justice demands . . . demands I be exposed.*

Joseph was thinking nothing of the kind. He could not
bring himself to cause Mary any more pain than what he
thought she was already suffering. He would divorce her by
going quietly before witnesses and write her a bill of divorce
without specifying the cause. Then he would make arrange-
ments to send her away from Nazareth until the baby was
born.

Weary with tossing and turning, in the fourth watch of the
night, Joseph finally fell asleep. With sleep came a dream, and
in the dream an angel appeared. "Joseph son of David," he said,
"do not be afraid to take Mary home as your wife, because what
is conceived in her is from the Holy Spirit. She will give birth
to a son, and you are to give him the name Jesus, because he
will save his people from their sins."

Only slowly did the truth sink in, and as it did Joseph began to understand something Isaiah had said. This is the way God's Word by the prophet Isaiah will be fulfilled: "The virgin will be with child and will give birth to a son, and they will call him Immanuel." *The name means "God with us,"* he remembered, and the meaning struck him with such force he had to get up and pace about the room.

Jacob, hearing him, roused up and asked sleepily, "Joseph?"

"All's well, father." And trying not to disturb him again, Joseph lay down.

For the next hour Joseph lay on his sleeping mat, going over and over in his mind what the angel had revealed. At the sound of the first cock crowing, he could stand it no longer, and flung off the covers. Not waiting for the sun to rise, he pulled on his clothes and went out in the dark to fetch Nathan.

When the news reached Mary that the wedding would take place she was so relieved that she cried. Salome flew into a frenzy, sewing far into the night, putting finishing touches on garments they'd been working on all winter. The stringing of beads and fastening of other ornaments busied the fingers of their friends.

"Make sure you keep plenty of oil on hand," Salome warned the girls. "It would be just like Joseph to come for Mary at midnight!"

"Not that sleepyhead," Mary, the wife of Clopas, said. "He works too hard to sit up late. You'll see, Mary."

Mary laughed. "A fine sister-in-law you are!"

Even though Joseph did come in the middle of the night he did not surprise Mary, who was dressed and waiting. Long before the procession reached the house Mary heard the men and roused her sister. "Salome, I think they're coming." They peeked out the door and saw the torches of the groomsmen who were coming on foot up the road. "I'll call the girls," Salome said, and rushed next door.

The friends came running, bringing commotion and giggling with them. Lighting their lamps, they nervously waited for the procession to arrive. "Do I look all right?" Mary asked repeatedly, and the excited girls examined every inch of the embroidered bridal gown to make sure it fit perfectly—straightened any wrinkles, smoothed her hair in back, and adjusted a strand of pearls.

"You look perfect!" Salome assured her, and kissing her cheek brought the veil down over Mary's face. All the women then hurried out into the courtyard.

Mary's old father, still sitting by the fire, told her, "You're the most beautiful bride in Nazareth." And with a twinkle in his eye, "As beautiful as your mother on her wedding day."

"Go, father, go," she urged him.

The old man laughed. "I'm going, I'm going," and opened the door. "Here they come. Joseph's on a camel!"

She took her father from the door and shooed him out back in the courtyard.

Left alone, Mary trembled in the darkness. A tiny crack in the door enabled her to watch the bridegroom approaching, escorted by his groomsmen bearing torches which lighted up the night. The poor beast was loaded down with ornaments, and Mary thought its rider never looked more handsome, bedecked as he was in his finest. Amidst the jovial crowd of well-wishers, Nathan coaxed the camel to its knees and held onto the haltar as Joseph climbed down. As Nathan tended the camel Joseph moved toward the house.

Mary quickly closed the door and waited for Joseph to open it. Her heart throbbing, she heard his footfalls, then the scrape of the latch as he lifted it. Opening the door he came inside, hesitated, then came closer. Slowly lifting the veil, he smiled as he studied her face. "In the name of God the merciful and gracious—this evening is blessed."

Quietly, she responded, "May God bless you."

Joseph, to be heard by the wedding party, shouted a glad cry of surprise, and the women and groomsmen outside took up the cry of joy. The rejoicing had begun!

Offering his arm, Joseph smiled down at Mary. "Shall we go?"

As they stepped outside cheers and applause greeted them. Then Mary's father and sister came forward to give their blessings. Salome spoke quietly, "My sister, may you increase to thousands upon thousands; may your offspring possess the gates of their enemies."

Then her father raised his hands in benediction, "The Lord bless you and keep you; the Lord make his face shine upon you and be gracious unto you; the Lord turn his face toward you and give you peace."

The solemnity ended, gaiety resumed and the young maidens, dancing to the jangle of tambourines, led the cortege back to Joseph's house. All along the route neighbors and friends joined the wedding party raising songs, laughing, ringing bells, and shouting. The noisy festivities continued as they reached the bridegroom's home. There a feast was prepared, and for hours they ate and drank while entertainers performed.

Such merry-making lasted seven days with people coming and going. By the time the last juggling act was performed, the last round of jests exchanged, Mary was exhausted. Taken to the wedding chamber by friends, she waited alone for Joseph to come. Escorted by the men, the bridegroom was left standing outside her door until the last of the well-wishers departed; then Joseph opened the door and entered the bridal room.

Together at last, Joseph took Mary in his arms. And holding her he said, "I'll not come near you, Mary . . . we'll not fulfill the marriage covenant until the child is born."

"As God wills," she murmured, and leaned her head against his chest.

Joseph stroked her hair, kissing the top of her head. "No one will know," he whispered.

7

Water to Wine

M ary, the mother of Jesus, went down to Cana to help her sister-in-law, who was also named Mary, with the wedding preparations. Clopas was on his way to the vineyard tower and hailed her. Seeing his worried face she asked him, "What's wrong?"

"Not much. I'm going to check the wine jars. Would you like to help me?" She followed him through the vineyard that lay along the sun-drenched slopes of the terraced hill. Stone walls held the soil from washing down the hillsides, and a watchman in the tower during harvest time kept robbers away. The tower rose to a height of forty feet with rooms for the man's family, but it was empty now that the season was over.

Here and there among the vines were jackal-scares made of whitewashed stones to the height of about three feet. Clopas complained, "We've had more grapes eaten by those fox-like jackals than by the harvesters."

Clopas's vines produced the luscious Hebron green-white grapes from which choice wine was made. He worked hard pruning and cultivating the vines and usually had a bountiful harvest. They passed the wine press hewn of solid rock and lined with mortar, where the grape gatherers dumped their basketsful to be trampled by barefoot servants. Mary could recall many happy days when grape harvest was celebrated, the festivities a highlight of the year, second only to the happy occasion of a wedding.

Entering the tower, Mary and Clopas found several Rhodian jars in the cool dark passageway that led to the floors above, their caps sealed with pitch. "It's hard for me to see," he said, and lit a lamp. "There. Will you hold it for me?"

Mary held the lamp so he could read the seals. Each pottery jar was stamped with the name of the magistrate and the year when the bottling was done. Examining one seal he shook his head. "It's not fully aged." So it was with the other one. "So much of the crop for the past few years has been fit only for making raisins," he explained. "Mary has some splendid pomegranate wine in the house. We'll serve that first. It's a favorite in Cana." He smiled. "Never let it be said that Clopas did not serve the best wine in the country."

As they walked back toward the house, Clopas told her the story of a neighbor whose son had been disgraced when the wine gave out at his wedding. "He has not shown his face in Cana since."

"I know. I heard about that in Nazareth."

"There's little danger that will happen to us. I don't think there'll be a big crowd—a number of families are going to Jerusalem for the feast. Your children are coming, aren't they?"

"The girls are busy, but Jesus is coming. My sister, Salome, and her husband, Zebedee, are on their way."

Clopas grew pensive. "I've heard some interesting things about that son of yours."

"You mean Jesus?" He nodded. "His baptism?" she asked.

"Yes. They say a voice was heard . . . the voice of God." He waited for an answer.

"That is what was told me."

"What do you make of it?"

"I must take it for what it is worth."

"You think he is the Son of God?"

They were nearing the house and his wife called to them. "Hurry," she yelled, "I need your help." When they reached the courtyard they saw she was having trouble trying to rotate the calf on the spit. Clopas came to her rescue and rolled the roasting calf on its other side. His wife laughed, "When I told you to fatten the calf, we'd need it for the wedding feast, I didn't mean *this* fat!"

The smell of the succulent meat, its juices sizzling, mingled with the odor of fresh-baked bread. "What's this?" Mary asked, lifting the lid of a pot. "Lentils and leeks?"

"Aye, lentils and leeks, James's favorite. And in this crock is the *leben*. I filled the crock yesterday with milk and leaven, covered it with this cloth—it should be setting nicely. We'll serve it, if not tonight, tomorrow." She looked at Clopas who, with the aid of the servants, was putting up the canopy in the courtyard. "Be sure you have the chickens and the lamb dressed for tomorrow. This veal will be devoured in no time at all."

"What about the fish?"

"The fourth day, remember? I told you yesterday."

"Did you make the raisin cakes?"

"I did." And, aside to Mary, she chuckled and whispered, "I hid them from him. He's like a child about raisin cakes!"

"Where's the bridegroom?"

"James was up in his room bathing a while ago. He should be dressing now. Oh, Mary, I can't wait for you to see him! The girdle he's wearing is of Syrian silk. And you know the alabaster of myrrh mother left me? I've given it to him, and his father gave him frankincense."

Wiping her hands on a towel she glanced about the courtyard, making sure everything was under control, then invited Mary to sit down under the awning. "I just have to get off my feet for a minute."

A breeze freshened the air and Mary welcomed the few minutes alone with her friend. "Is James nervous?"

"I'd say so," his mother replied, "though he tries to hide it. He's very serious, you know, so afraid his bride will find fault with him—as if anyone could find fault with *my* son . . . Such presents he gave her! A beautiful veil, a fine comb, a sash, and a ring. But then, she gave to him as well—a prayer shawl and

a silver chain." She looked Mary up and down. "You're griev-
ing still, aren't you?"

"I suppose. Ever since Joseph died—"

"Ah, Joseph. We miss him. When I think how he would've
enjoyed these days now that Jesus—Jesus is coming to the
wedding, isn't he?"

"Oh, yes. He's down at Nathanael's house with some
friends."

"Speaking of Joseph, we often think of Zacharias and Elizabeth, too. I wonder what they would think of John now that
he's causing such a stir."

"They would not be surprised, I'd say."

"Oh?"

"I don't suppose John's coming for the wedding."

"No. He's not a man to socialize. We haven't seen him for
quite a while, but the last time I saw him he looked . . . well,
eccentric. Living in the desert, his skin was like a goat's hide,
and his beard looked as if it'd never been trimmed. He always
wears a hair coat from a camel and survives on food he finds
in the wild. I can't imagine him coming to a wedding."

Clopas came past them, giving instructions to the servants:
"Make sure the jars for foot-washing are filled—see that you
fill the cistern, too." He went through the house onto the
street.

"He's probably looking to see if Zebedee and Salome are
coming up the road. Do you think their sons will come?"

"John's coming. He's with Jesus now, but James will probably stay home to fish."

"Who else is with Jesus?"

"Philip, Andrew, and his brother Simon." Mary felt the
nagging worry again. "Mary," she confided, "I'm concerned
about Jesus."

"Yes, I heard."

"You heard about his fasting?"

"Forty days, wasn't it?"

"Forty days."

"He lost weight?"

"I didn't see him right away; when I did, he didn't seem the worse for it."

"Why do you worry?"

"It's something the Baptist said. Andrew told me that when Jesus finished fasting, John saw him coming from the desert—"

"So?"

Mary hesitated. "John called him the lamb of God."

"*The lamb of God?* What do you think he meant by that?"

"I'm not sure . . . Do you think—"

Clopas was shouting. "Here they come!"

The two women jumped up to greet the approaching guests. The women, embracing, jabbering like magpies, left the men to themselves. Ushering the women inside, Mary called back over her shoulder to her husband. "Clopas, don't you think you'd better get dressed?"

Zebedee called after the women, "Salome, where'd you put my wedding garment?"

"It's in the pouch, right where you put it!"

"The governor of the feast will be here any minute, Clopas," his wife told him, urging him to hurry. "Have him taste the wine before you bring it to the house."

"He's here now," he replied, and they saw Malcham coming in the door. A portly man with poor vision, he always had a stressful look about him. Making quick work of salutations, he inspected the meal being prepared and approved the arrangement of places around the triclinium—the low table around which the guests, in the absence of couches, would sit or squat on the floor. The table was on the platform above the floor where the lesser guests were to sit.

Malcham was a meticulous man, not to be deterred. Clopas unsealed the pomegranate wine first, gave him a sip, and watched Malcham as he enjoyed the taste, rolling his eyes and smacking his lips. Then Clopas called a servant to bring a jug from the tower in case it was needed later. "We've enough of the pomegranate, I think, but just in case—"

Satisfied that all was in order, Malcham sat down in the courtyard to await the coming event. The bridegroom's brother Joseph and several friends were gathering outside, dressed in wedding finery, and from their jocular remarks they were caught up in a celebrating spirit.

The women made sure the food was cooking properly; that the eggs, figs, and pickled olives were ready for serving. Then they retired to dress while the men were getting ready in James's room.

By the time the women were all properly attired the men were waiting for them in the courtyard, James in their center. He was a spindly youth, self-conscious and awkward, yet Mary thought he had never looked better.

"How handsome you are," his mother said. "Here, let me fix your crown . . ." And fussing with the wreath, "These flowers look wilted . . . There, now, that's better." She turned to Mary and Salome. "Didn't I tell you he looks like a prince?"

James blushed at his mother's extravagance. "I must be going, woman."

The good-natured banter of his friends made the bridegroom blush the more.

Disregarding her son's discomfort, his mother boasted to the other women, "I embroidered the sleeves. Feel this girdle, Salome. Have you ever felt finer silk? See the threads of gold and silver woven in?" She spoke to James. "Are your sandals laced carefully?" and raised the flowing robes to see. Satisfied that they were, she dropped the skirts, kissed him good-bye. "Your perfume is as fragrant as a garden in springtime."

As James and his friends set out for the bride's home, Mary and the other women followed. They reached the house just as the family were giving their benedictions. The girl was several years younger than James, perhaps fifteen or less. Her lovely face had the luster of marble, smooth and soft, and her dark hair was braided with pearls and other precious stones

borrowed from neighbors. A brilliant jewel adorned her forehead and there were ornaments hanging from her ears and
dress.

As they began the procession back to the bridegroom's
home, as tradition required the girl let down her hair and let
it fall loose about her shoulders. People along the way joined
the well-wishers, among them Jesus and five of his friends.
Torches flaming, the paraders singing, throwing parched
grain to the children along the way, James brought his bride
home.

When they reached the house Mary and Salome under-
took the task of rearranging the bride's hair, hiding her locks
beneath a thick veil. When they finished the bride rejoined
the bridegroom, and the village rabbi met the bridal pair
under the canopy. There he blessed them with words once
spoken to Boaz: "May the Lord make the woman who is
coming into your home like Rachel and Leah, who together
built up the house of Israel." And the guests responded, "We
are witnesses." Blessing a cup of wine, the rabbi handed it to
James who sipped of it and, in turn, held it for his bride to
drink. A burst of applause followed the taking of the wine,
and the couple moved inside the house for the wedding feast
to begin.

As the guests entered they paused at the door to let servants
wash their feet, then took their places. As more and more
people gathered in the room Mary, looking worried, whispered to her husband, "Clopas, how many do you think are
here?"

He shook his head. "Far more than we expected."

The seats of honor on the platform were reserved for the
wedding party. When Jesus and his disciples entered they took
the lower seats, but right away Jesus was ushered onto the
platform and placed beside Clopas.

Just as he reached the table a ruffian came barging in the
door. A loud remonstrance followed, and the governor of the
feast was quickly informed. Malcham called out to the servants.

"Tell him he can't come in here. He doesn't have on a wedding garment." And to those at the table, "He knows better than that."

The servants made quick work of evicting the intruder. To divert attention from the incident while they waited for the meal to be served, Malcham called for the entertainer whose specialty was riddles.

The meal was served one course at a time, the food in a common bowl placed where guests could reach it. Malcham gave thanks and offered a benediction upon the couple. Then he dipped a piece of flat bread into the lentils and served the morsel to the bridegroom. Receiving the sop, James was careful not to dribble bean juice on his robe and washed down the mouthful with the sweet pomegranate wine.

The leisurely meal was interspersed with dancing—men with men, clapping hands in rhythm to the pipes and moving in a snakelike fashion in a circle—women singing and swaying in time with the music. With much coming and going, in the free and easy spirit of the occasion, there was much laughter and singing and no end to mirthful ballads and old vintage songs.

In the midst of everything that was going on, a young zealot named Simon carried on a heated discussion about revolt against Rome. When arguing threatened the happy occasion, Malcham was quick to offer another blessing for the bridal pair and direct attention to the purpose of the celebration.

They were well into the week's festivities when the pomegranate wine gave out, and the inferior *tirosh* from the tower was being served. Clopas was worried. "Next we'll have to give them vinegar."

Mary looked at her son, turning over in her mind what Jesus might do should the wine give out. Since the death of Joseph she had come to depend on her eldest son, who was always willing to help. Even so, Mary knew she had no hold on him. Ever since Jesus was a child she had stood in awe of him, knowing he must be about his Father's business. As Joseph had often reminded her, Isaiah called the virgin-born "Immanuel," *God with us,* something neither of them quite knew how to reckon with.

As the feast continued wine was rationed by scant servings, but even so it did not last. A servant came to Clopas and whispered something in his ear. From Clopas's anguished look Mary knew the wine was all gone. Leaning over to Jesus she whispered, "They have no more wine."

He looked back at her kindly. "Dear woman, why do you involve me? My time has not yet come."

Mary did not disregard what he said, but knowing Jesus she thought he would do something to relieve the distress. When two of the servants came near she beckoned to them. "Do whatever he tells you."

The men took up positions nearby, waiting to be summoned. In a little while Jesus was ready to give instructions.

Near the door stood six stone water jars used in washing feet. Jesus told the servants, "Fill the jars with water." They bowed politely and made their way through the crowded room.

It took them quite a while to haul enough water from the cistern to fill the jars, for each one contained twenty to thirty gallons, and they were careful to fill them to the brim. By then, guests were asking for more wine. Jesus pushed through the revelers and stood beside the water pots as the last one was filled. To the servants he said, "Now draw some out and take it to the master of the banquet."

The bewildered men were dumbfounded. Mary also questioned what he was asking, and thought, *No one serves* water *to drink.* But she watched as the servants poured, and as they poured the water turned to wine! Astonished, her mouth dropped open. The amazed servants stared first at the cup, then at Jesus—until one of them slowly raised the cup to his nose, smelled the aroma, and closing his eyes savored it.

Another servant scolded him, "Stand aside. The master of the feast tastes first."

Malcham paid little notice to the wine set before him until he lifted it to his lips. No sooner did he take a mouthful than he raised his eyebrows in surprise. Sipping thoughtfully, he showed increasing delight, and when the cup was drained he motioned for the servant to fill it again. With the wine in hand he got up from the table and, touching the bridegroom on the shoulder, asked, "May I see you outside?"

Moving out of earshot from the other guests, Malcham said to James, "Everyone brings out the choice wine first and then the cheaper wine after the guests have had too much to drink; but you have saved the best till now."

James shrugged his shoulders. "I thought the first was best—it was that good pomegranate wine we prefer."

"Taste this," Malcham said, and with the first swallow James exclaimed, "I've never tasted wine like this. I've never tasted anything this good!"

Malcham gave the servants the go-ahead signal and, as they served the wine to other guests, comments began to be made all around the room. "Clopas, did you make this wine?" "What flavor! Are these Hebron grapes?"

At first only the servants knew the source of the wine. But during the remaining days of the feast, as they continued drinking and asking questions, others learned that Jesus had made the wine. The miracle convinced his disciples and they put their faith in him.

8

Catching a Multitude of Fish

GO AWAY FROM ME, LORD; I AM A SINFUL MAN!

Scripture Reference: John 3:1–21; 4; Luke 5:1–11

A ndrew wasn't paying attention and, from the way the net was draped over his arm, Simon Peter knew the cast would become tangled; but he couldn't tell Andrew anything, so he kept quiet. They were both tired from working all night, and this casting of the nets along the shore was a last resort, unwilling as they were to admit failure. In water teeming with fish they had caught nothing all night long, although they had sailed clear across the lake dragging the net back and forth. Now they were on the northwest shore at Tabgha near the Seven Springs. *If we can't catch anything here, we might as well give up,* Peter thought, *because these are the best fishing grounds anywhere on the lake.*

The sea was ruffled by the wind, and heavy mists still hovered over the water in the predawn light. Whitecaps splashing against the jetty projecting out from shore seemed as irritable as the fishermen. Peter waded in water up to his waist before he cast his net, whirling it expertly so that it fell in a circle as it sank to the bottom. Then he dived down, closed the bottom, and pulled the net ashore.

Just as he expected, he didn't catch anything edible, only one small sheet fish and some unscaled creature. He tossed them back and looked to see how Andrew was doing. Sure enough, Andrew's net was tangled, and he was sitting down fumbling with the weights and floats trying to get the net free.

Peter called it a day. Walking past the boats they had

beached, he joined Zebedee's men and dropped his net in the pile to be washed. If there was anything he hated to do it was to wash nets, particularly when he had nothing to show for his work. Picking off the slimy plant and marine life was a disagreeable task and, hungry as he was, he put off tackling the job. Reclining on his elbows before the fire, he watched John and James examining the nets for torn places. As one was washed and mended, it was slung over a yardarm or the side of a boat to dry, and Peter counted them. *Good*, he thought, *they're nearly done.*

Wearily, Peter watched the changing colors in the sky as the sun rose behind the hills. The water was calmer now, and reflections from the sky turned the sea a pale gold. A crow, caw-cawing its way across the lake, announced the coming of the day.

The servants were arguing about why they hadn't caught anything, one thinking it was the wrong time of the moon, another that the east wind was blowing. Peter knew only that their nets were empty and he was tired of explanations. They had counted on this catch—John had promised the high priest in Jerusalem a load of fish by the end of the week, and Zebedee kept reminding them they must salt down some bream and carp to ship to Roman ports. *We've given it our best try*, Peter thought, *even given up following the Master to concentrate on business for a while.*

Ever since that day Andrew had hurried home with the news he'd found the Messiah, Simon Peter had felt he wanted to be a part of the company that followed Jesus of Nazareth. He remembered with satisfaction the name Jesus gave him, "Cephas" or "Rock," and he liked to think of himself as sturdy as a rock—though often he doubted that he would ever be so stable. He thought back to the year before when, in Cana, Jesus had turned water to wine. That miracle had convinced him that Jesus was a man to be believed; and hearing all that John the Baptist had to say about him, Peter was increasingly interested in finding out more.

He rubbed the hard calluses on his palm and wished he had more schooling. He had never been one to sit still and listen to a teacher, preferring rather to be outside in the wind and weather doing things. The fact that Jesus was not like the Capernaum rabbi, whose nose was in the scrolls all the time, made the Master more approachable.

Yet Jesus was not afraid of the intelligentsia. Peter had to laugh when he thought of it—one man single-handedly chasing out those robbers in the Temple, throwing over their money-changing tables—driving the animals into the street! What a day that had been!

John said the intelligentsia were so impressed one of them came to see Jesus—one of the Sanhedrin, in fact—a man named Nicodemus. Peter wondered what they talked about. Jesus probably told Nicodemus the same things he told that Samaritan woman at Jacob's well, but Peter didn't know for sure what that conversation was about either. Nevertheless, he had a good idea what they talked about after the two days they spent with the Samaritans in Sychar.

Another crow was crossing the lake, cawing after its mate. The sun was dissipating the fog, drawing it up and warming it away. Peter shaded his eyes with his hand. Down on the beach the nobleman's son was skipping stones on the flat surface of the lake. His father was busy in Capernaum and had put the boy in charge of servants, who brought him to the lake to play in the sun. Although he was perfectly healthy now that Jesus had healed him, it was thought the sun and air would be good for him. The boy was as bronze as a seafaring man and full of mischief.

Healing the boy was only one of the wonderful things Jesus had done, and Peter couldn't understand why the Galileans were opposing him. Opposition in Judea was understandable, because the religious leaders felt threatened by the Master's teaching; but only recently, in Jesus' own hometown, he had been rejected. During a Sabbath service Jesus had been asked to speak, and when he claimed to fulfill a prophecy of Isaiah's about the Messiah, the townspeople rose up in arms and would have pushed him over the cliff. He escaped and left Nazareth, perhaps for good. Now he was living in Capernaum.

Well, Peter thought, *I must get up and go to work.* Carrying the hand net to the trough, he soused it several times and began the task of picking off the bits and pieces of debris. In a little while he heard John calling him. He turned to see him pointing down the beach. Peter gazed in that direction; a lot of people were gathered along the shore about a hundred yards away. At first he thought they were looking for fish to buy, then he realized there were too many of them for that. There was an attraction of some kind.

"Is that Jesus?" John yelled.

Peter stood on his tiptoes trying to see. "I don't see him," he answered. Watching the crowd moving along the shore he guessed it must be Jesus, for he could think of nothing else that would draw people out so early in the morning.

As they came nearer he knew it was Jesus, for he saw the top of his head. Tired as he was, the sight of Jesus gave Peter a happy feeling; and when he saw how the crowd was mobbing him, bombarding him with requests, Peter wanted to send them all away that he might have the Master to himself.

As the crowd came alongside Peter's boat Jesus raised his hand above their heads, and Peter understood he was trying to get his attention. Standing on his tiptoes he craned his neck to catch Jesus' eye. Jesus motioned toward the boat then thumbed toward the sea, asking him to put out a little from the shore.

Peter called Andrew who came running to help him shove the craft back into the water. When it was afloat Jesus came aboard and took a seat. There he was out of the reach of the people and could address them in an orderly way. When the boat had eased a little distance from land, Andrew let down the anchor.

Jesus waited for the people to settle down. Some of them

sat on the beach, others squatted down. When they were quiet he began speaking. Peter was disappointed in his story. Jesus was talking about a sower, and farming was something he was not interested in; his mind drifted to the children playing in the shallow water near shore. Beneath the clear water were pebbles or shells that caught the morning light in such a way they seemed like jewels, but the children were for making sand houses, muddying the water and obscuring the exquisite stones.

A flock of crows was passing overhead and Peter followed them with his eye until they were out of sight. He pitied the poor farmer on whose crop they would alight.

The muscles in Peter's back were sore from the long hours of casting and rowing, and he was so hungry he hoped Jesus would not talk much longer. He needed to get home, have something to eat, and try to sleep a few hours before they'd have to set out to sea again.

His reverie was interrupted; Jesus was speaking to him. "Put out into deep water, and let down the nets for a catch."

Peter looked at him questioningly, unwilling to commit the clean nets to the sea, but Andrew started pulling up the anchor. Reluctantly, Peter took to the oars and headed the little craft toward deeper water. As he rowed his eyes rested on the dragnets hanging from the yardarm, and he inwardly groaned to think he'd have to wash them again before he could call it a day. *If I were a rich man*, he thought, *I'd never wash another net, just let them rot.*

When they reached deep water Peter stopped rowing and let the boat idle. "Master," he said, hesitating, "we've worked hard all night and haven't caught anything." Seeing Jesus wasn't going to change his mind, Peter added, "But because you say so, I will let down the nets."

With Jesus looking on Peter and Andrew slung the net in a far-flung arc and watched it land with a slight splash. Soon the floats aligned themselves on either side and the fishermen prepared another net to cast.

With both nets in the water Andrew hoisted the sail, and the little craft moved lazily in the morning breeze. Impatient, Peter motioned his brother to bring in the nets.

They began to do so, straining with all their might, but the weight of the catch was so heavy they couldn't haul it in! Peter felt the net giving way in places, and he realized they'd never get the catch aboard without help. He shouted and with one hand frantically sent distress signals to James and John. Over his shoulder he saw them running for their boat, saw them shoving it in the water. Working frenziedly to save the catch Peter, with his foot against the side of the ship, braced himself. Andrew, red in the face, the veins in his neck distended, was straining to hang on, and Peter feared the other boat might not reach them in time.

Yet, in the stress, uppermost in his mind was Jesus. *This is God's power! Jesus is the Lord! We are in the presence of God!* And an overpowering conviction of sin took hold of him. He could not wait to be free from the work at hand!

At last the other boat drew alongside, and as it jockeyed for position Andrew directed James and John to grab the other side of the net. As they did Peter and Andrew lifted the net on their side, letting the flip-flopping fish slide into their partners' boat. Peter could see the other craft sinking lower in the water as the weight of the fish increased—when it went below the water mark the fishermen reversed the process and began filling Peter's boat. As the slippery fish piled deeper and deeper, Peter felt the boat sinking dangerously lower in the water. By the time the net was empty neither craft could bear the weight of another fish! The men, astonished at what they were witnessing, couldn't believe their eyes!

Simon Peter, conscience-stricken, stumbled through the pile of fish and fell down at Jesus' knees crying, "Go away from me, Lord; I am a sinful man!"

Feeling miserably unworthy, it was all he knew to say, but

he knew Jesus would never abandon a broken-hearted sinner.

Jesus reached out to him. "Don't be afraid," he said, "from now on you will catch men."

Simon Peter bowed his head, hiding the tears streaming down his face, and Andrew headed for shore.

Seeing what had happened, Zebedee's servants rushed out to meet them and brought both boats up on land. While they unloaded the fish, Jesus spoke to the four. "Come, follow me and I will make you fishers of men."

Immediately James and John went to speak with their father. In a few minutes they returned, ready to follow Jesus. "Leaving your nets?" Andrew asked.

"Everything," James replied.

"We are too," Simon Peter told them.

The servants, having observed all that went on, looked appalled, but not one of the four fishermen looked back—not at the lucrative catch of fish, nor their prize boats, nor their family and friends—as they fell in step with Jesus.

9

A Cripple Healed at Bethesda

STOP SINNING OR SOMETHING WORSE MAY HAPPEN TO YOU.

Scripture Reference: John 5

Jerusalem was thronged with people celebrating the feast. As John followed Jesus from the Temple, they were headed toward the Sheep Gate, the one farthest east on the northern wall. He knew they would wind up at the "House of Grace," as Bethesda was called, and he didn't care to be going there. By the Sheep Gate were pools fed by an erratic spring. Superstitious people believed an angel came down at times and stirred the water; whoever was first in the water would be cured. The "pool cures" were far from convincing, and John did not enjoy seeing the sick and suffering lying about waiting with false hope for the moving of the water.

But Jesus was determined to go there. As they reached the colonnades that sheltered the sick and dying John heard one old woman screaming, a tired, monotonous crying; and from the disregard of the other sick people he knew her crying must be continuous. Her cavernous eyes held a vacant stare as if no mind existed, and the deformities of her limbs appeared to be set in stone. He wondered that she had lived so long.

There were two colonnades on either side with one in the middle separating the two pools. A twenty-foot rock partition lay between them, and it was on that partition John saw a wretched man whose legs were covered with raw ulcers. Positioned to roll off the edge should the water move, he was being constantly harassed by a maimed one who could not crawl so near. Yet the dullness with which the man on the partition regarded his persecutor revealed his hopelessness.

The smell of unwashed bodies and the filth of the place nearly made John gag. Everywhere he looked were scores of the moaning, groaning, miserable ill whose conditions were incurable.

There was a paralyzed youth, his mother holding his head in her lap, his eyes bright with fever as he babbled incoherently. A blind woman, perhaps mute as well, trailed her fingers in the water and hummed to herself. He knew from past experience that their faces would linger in his mind, their pitiful pleas sound in his ears for weeks to come. Unless, of course, Jesus healed them. It was the Sabbath and should he heal anyone it would surely cause a furor.

Still following the Master as he picked his way among the listless forms, John wondered if Jesus was searching for someone in particular. They came upon a cripple John had known as long as he had had a house in Jerusalem. When Jesus inquired John told him the man had not always lain at the pool, but for thirty-eight years he had been an invalid. He was a man of bad reputation, although John could not remember his offence. From his appearance he looked like a glutton.

Jesus asked him, "Do you want to get well?"

John thought the question superfluous until he heard the man's reply. "Sir, I have no one to help me into the pool when the water is stirred. While I am trying to get in, someone else goes down ahead of me."

To John the answer sounded more like an excuse than a reason. *In all the time he's lain there, surely someone would have helped him,* John reasoned. *It looks like he would have a friend— someone. Is he so despicable he doesn't have a friend? Of course, he weighs a ton . . . And it's true that at Bethesda it's every man for himself.*

He caught himself. *It's silly to think like this—it wouldn't cure him if he did get in the water first.*

John studied the cripple carefully and wondered if he were

the kind of man who enjoyed being sick. He'd known people like that. There was a whine in the man's voice that sounded like self-pity.

Then John reproached himself, *I know I shouldn't judge.*

Jesus spoke in a commanding voice as the man looked up at him. "Get up! Pick up your mat and walk."

The command startled the cripple but he got up, rolled up his mat, and walked about!

John was so excited about seeing the man walk that he scarcely thought about the Jewish disapproval of carrying a burden on the Sabbath. When he did think of it, he tried to dismiss the fear.

Jesus quickly slipped through the porches littered with the sick and suffering and left the "House of Grace." As John followed him he was troubled. *I wonder why he didn't heal all of them,* he puzzled. *Is it because he doesn't want to bring down the wrath of the Jews . . . No, that's not it. If he wanted to avoid the wrath of the Jews he wouldn't risk healing anyone on the Sabbath.*

In the afternoon of the same day they went to the Temple, where the noise in the court precinct was always deafening. Above the hubbub of people milling about were the screaming voices of people shouting about the high prices for sacrificial lambs and others angrily arguing with money changers. The lowing of cattle and baa-ing of sheep added to the din, and the place smelled like a barnyard.

In the confusion of that crowded place Jesus found the healed cripple again and spoke to him. "See, you are well again. Stop sinning or something worse may happen to you."

So, it was true, thought John. *It was the man's own fault that he had been sick. Was it overindulgence of some kind, or was his disease the result of another sin?*

The man learned Jesus' name, and as he left John suspected he might be going to the authorities to identify Jesus as his healer. That made John nervous, for Jerusalem teemed with Sabbath-keeping legalists.

Sure enough, as soon as the healed man reported to the Jews they came accusing Jesus, persecuting him. Jesus answered their accusation straightforwardly, asserting that it is wrong not to do good on the Sabbath, for so God works. "My Father is always at his work to this very day, and I, too, am working."

Jesus' words infuriated the accusers, particularly because he made himself equal with God, and there was angry talk of killing him. The threat did not intimidate him—Jesus proceeded to give them a discourse on his relationship with the Father; his authority to give eternal life; and lambasted them for disobeying Moses and not having the love of God in their hearts!

When the long day finally came to a close John reflected on the healing of a man who did not so much as ask to be healed, one who had nothing to recommend him to God's mercy. Compared to the other sick people at Bethesda, he was no worse off—why, then, did Jesus heal him and not the others?

It was not a question he felt he could put to the Lord. And although he pondered it for some time, in the end he had to satisfy himself with the sure knowledge that some of the ways of God are inscrutable.

10

Legion

GO HOME TO YOUR FAMILY AND TELL THEM HOW MUCH
THE LORD HAS DONE FOR YOU . . .

Scripture Reference: Mark 5:1–20; Matthew 8:28–34; Luke 8:26–39

Philip half-reclined near the prow of the ship and gazed out over the tranquil sea. Only an hour before the vessel had been in the worst storm he had ever experienced in all the years he'd been a fisherman on the Sea of Galilee. The deck was still wet from the waves that had crashed over the sides, and not a man aboard was yet recovered from the astonishing miracle that had taken place. Jesus simply spoke to the wind and waves, commanded them to be still, and the wind stopped blowing and the waves became calm.

Although Philip and the others felt euphoric that all was well and by such an extraordinary means, the experience had drained them emotionally, and they looked forward to some rest and relaxation when they reached shore. As a native of Bethsaida Philip knew a great deal about Decapolis, the region where they were headed. Few Jews lived there, and the Greek inhabitants were less likely to be interested in Jesus, less likely to be making demands upon him. He and the disciples should have a few days of relative solitude there.

Gadara was the one city among the ten in the district of Decapolis that Philip would most like to visit. The town was large and, perched on a headland a few miles southeast from the Sea of Galilee, it enjoyed a magnificent view of the sea. The Yarmuk river ran between the city and the sea, and north of the river were the hot springs where Philip hoped he might soak his tired body.

In Gadara were two theaters where orators and actors performed, but Philip cared little for orators and actors. They were a vain lot, and what they had to say was beyond a fisherman's concern.

The beach was clearly visible now, and the Twelve were moving about, getting ready to bring the ship to shore. Philip could see some herdsman on the crest of the hill. *They don't look like shepherds,* he thought. *I don't see sheep. Maybe they're tending goats. No, not goats. Pigs.*

Dark holes marked the limestone tombs carved from the hillside along the shore, and Philip thought about the human wretches rumored to live there. He had once talked to a Greek fisherman who told him townspeople had tried every means of coercion and restraint to control the wild men who claimed the tombs, but to no avail. Night and day the demon-possessed roamed about, crying out, cutting themselves with stones. The Greek claimed the possessed could break chains with their supernatural strength.

As the boat drew nearer shore Philip heard something. "What's that?" he asked.

"Sounds like a madman," Matthew said.

As the ship drifted closer the two stood looking ashore, trying to see where the unearthly screaming was coming from. The anchor was being lowered and, when the vessel was secured, Philip climbed over the side of the ship and dropped into the water with the rest of the men. As they waded ashore the bloodcurdling screams grew louder. As they walked onto the beach they saw two figures leaving a cave—two naked men, their bodies bruised and bleeding. One of them came running down the hill waving his arms and shrieking. Jesus went to meet him, commanding the demon, "Come out of this man, you evil spirit!" and the madman fell on his knees before Jesus, yelling at the top of his voice, "What do you want with me, Jesus, Son of the Most High God? Swear to God that you won't torture me!"

Philip stayed close by Matthew, afraid of the raging maniac.

"He wants us to get out of his territory, Matthew."

Jesus was asking the man, "What is your name?"

"My name is Legion," he screamed, "for we are many."

Matthew looked at Philip. "What does he mean?"

"He means he has so many demons in him they'd make a legion."

"A legion can mean six thousand men!"

"I know," Philip said, "but look at him!" Emaciated, cuts and bruises all over his body, his wrists and ankles encircled with broken manacles, it was not hard to believe thousands of demons tormented him.

The man was begging Jesus not to send the demons out of the area. In a high, shrieking, unnatural voice, the demons were pleading, "Send us among the pigs; allow us to go into them."

Jesus granted the request, and instantly the herd of swine was squealing, maddened by the evil spirits. Panic-stricken they stampeded down the hill, plunging into the sea!

Philip and Matthew started running up the hill to get a better view. The herdsmen were scattering in all directions to get out of the way of the pigs thundering past. The pigs headed straight for the sea and were drowning. "What'll we do?" a swineherd shouted, "We'll lose the whole drove!"

"How many is that?" Philip asked.

"Two thousand!"

"Two thousand pigs?"

"You heard me!" he yelled, and snatching up his cloak he called to his fellows, "Come on! We must report this right away!"

As the keepers ran toward town Philip and Matthew went back down the hill where the disciples were helping the healed man bathe. Submerged in water, he was washing blood and grime from his limbs, so happy he was laughing and crying at the same time. Nathanael scrubbed his matted hair and beard. When the bathing was finished, he waded ashore, dried himself on a linen towel, then wrapped it around his waist. Still laughing and crying for joy, he seemed almost beside himself; but the light of reason was in his eyes and there was no mistaking his restored sanity. Thomas found undergarments somewhere, and helped him put them on. James held a shirt for him to pull over his head, and Matthew went back to the ship to fetch a cloak.

"These manacles, how can we get them off?" James asked.

"There's a crowbar on board," Andrew said, and yelled to Matthew, "Bring the crowbar."

"And the file," Thomas added.

Simon Peter reached inside a knapsack and pulled out two loaves of bread and a smoked fish. Someone had wine. "Let the man eat," he said. "He must be starved."

The excited man devoured the food, washed it down with the wine, and nervously picked and ate the crumbs down the front of his cloak so as not to waste them.

Philip thought he heard voices, and looking up he saw a number of men coming over the hill. "Uh-oh. They must be the owners."

When the men saw the carcasses floating in the sea they stopped, and the herdsmen pointed back and forth from the pigs to the disciples on shore. Storming down the hill their voices loud and angry, the irate men headed straight for Jesus. Then they saw the formerly demon-possessed man sitting down, clothed, and in his right mind! They stopped dead in their tracks.

Thomas was filing an iron shackle from an ankle and both men were so absorbed with the task, they did not look up. The owners stared, nonplussed as to what to do or say. In a few minutes they withdrew to discuss the matter.

An argument ensued but eventually they reached an agreement. When they came back their spokesman addressed Jesus, entreating him to leave their shores.

Good, Philip thought, *they don't accuse us of destroying their property. Even they know the cost of animal life is of no concern when a man's health is at stake . . . Or, do they? . . . Maybe they're Jews and know they're sinning in raising swine.*

Jesus agreed to leave and told the others to gather up their belongings. Philip was disappointed; he was looking forward to some time in the region of Gadara. Thomas, having pried off the last manacle, handed him the crowbar, and Philip turned to follow Jesus back to the ship.

Looking up the shore where the dead pigs littered the beach, Philip thought, *I wonder what becomes of the demons now.*

Just as they were about to climb in the boat, their new friend came splashing after them, begging Jesus to let him go with them. Jesus shook his head and, seeing the man's dismay, told him, "Go home to your family and tell them how much the Lord has done for you, and how he has had mercy on you."

For a moment he looked downcast. Then his face brightened at the prospect, and obediently he bid them farewell and waded back ashore.

Philip busied himself unfurling the sail as the boat moved slowly out to sea. The herdsmen and owners were strewn up and down the shore, assessing their losses, while the one Jesus had delivered stood on the beach waving good-bye to those on board.

Wind caught the sail causing the small craft to pick up speed, and rapidly they put distance between themselves and the shore. As they sailed briskly away, Philip watched the happy man running up the hill, heading home. Philip wondered if he would ever see the man again.

11

The Hungry Fed

SURELY THIS IS THE PROPHET WHO IS TO COME INTO THE
WORLD.

Scripture Reference: John 6:1–14, Matthew 14:15–21;

Mark 6:32–44; Luke 9:12–17

The apostles had just returned from a mission tour and
were so busy with people coming and going, they did
not have a chance to eat. Then came the devastating news from
Tiberias: John the Baptist had been beheaded by Herod Anti-
pas to satisfy the cruel desire of Herodias, his wife. John's
disciples buried his body then came and told Jesus.

When the news was received in Capernaum, because the
people considered John to be a prophet there was danger of an
uprising. There was also fear that Herod might try to kill Jesus.

The Lord got up and headed for the ship, saying to his
disciples, "Come with me by yourselves to a quiet place and
get some rest."

As they were putting out to sea Philip looked back and saw
a crowd gathering on the pier, watching after them. "Look,"
he said to Simon the Zealot, "they're likely to follow us."

Sure enough, some of the followers were beginning to run
on foot around the lake. "It's ten miles around the north end,
six across," he said. "With the wind against us I daresay they'll
be waiting for us when we reach the other side."

"Some of those people are going to the Feast of Passover
in Jerusalem, Philip."

The rough water bounced the boat around, slapping it this way and that, and all the apostles were busy keeping the craft on course. For several hours there was no relaxing on board, and then they saw their destination come into view.

Philip watched the chalk and basalt hills on the other side loom larger as the boat drew steadily closer. The eastern hills were as high as a thousand feet, much higher than the hills on the western side, and the table land was cut up with valleys. Desolate, it was an ideal location for solitude, and the sweet spring air promised good weather.

But when they were closer Simon nudged him. "Look yonder." And Philip saw people swarming on the beach. "Philip, do you suppose some of them are pilgrims returning from the Feast of Purim?"

Judas Iscariot spoke up. "Yes, but I'll bet most of them are waiting for more miracles, such as they've seen before. There'll be all kinds of moaning, groaning cripples—sick, blind—"

There goes our rest, Philip thought, and Simon, exasperated, shook his head. The men rested on the oars, letting the boat glide onto the shallows as they studied the crowd on shore. Peter was watching Jesus, and speaking more to himself than to the others, said, "He sees them as sheep without a shepherd."

When the hull of the boat scraped bottom the disciples hopped out, and secured the craft while Jesus waded ashore.

Sure enough, Jesus immediately began healing the sick among them. When he was done with healing he beckoned to the disciples to follow him up on the mountain. When they reached a safe distance from the multitude, Jesus sat down to instruct them privately. The sermon on that mount was one Philip did not fully understand but one he would never forget. Stored in his mind were all Jesus' words to be recovered at a more convenient time, meditated upon.

As they came down from the mountain the multitude was still waiting patiently, and Jesus repeated to them much of what he had told the disciples.

Philip watched the sun slowly descending in the west, and wondered when and what they would eat. Simon the Zealot was apparently thinking the same thoughts. "Don't you think we'd better dismiss the crowd so they can go find something to eat?"

Philip wondered where so many people could find food in such a remote area. "I'd say there are roughly five thousand men and who knows how many women and children."

"They should get going before night overtakes them," Simon said. "Let's go see Jesus."

Together, they went to Jesus and explained the situation. "This is a remote place," they said, "and it's already very late. Send the people away so they can go to the surrounding countryside and villages and buy themselves something to eat."

But the Lord answered them, "You give them something to eat."

Philip was dumbfounded. Pushed aside by the crowd, he tried to find a place where he could sit down, collect his thoughts, and try to come up with something. Finding none, he waded out to the boat and climbed aboard. Simon followed him.

Sitting down in the stern, he studied the mob spread out as far as the eye could see. Figuring in his head, he considered how much it would cost to give them the merest snack. The average daily wage for a farm worker was one *denarius.* Philip started with that figure. With one *denarius* he could buy ten quarts of wheat or thirty quarts of barley. With two hundred *denarii* he could buy two thousand quarts of wheat or six thousand quarts of barley. That would not furnish soldiers' rations which, in the Greek army, was one quart of wheat a day, but it would provide a little. One-third of that would feed five thousand men one meal. The other two-thirds, divided among the women and children, might feed them a meal as well. "Two hundred *denarii* is more than we could possibly raise," he told Simon. "And even if we could find that much money among us, there's no place to buy food around here. Whatever does Jesus mean, 'You give them something to eat'?"

"I say we need a Moses to pray down manna," Simon said.

"Or an Elisha."

"Elisha?"

"Don't you remember? Elisha fed a hundred men with twenty loaves of bread."

"No, I don't remember that. A hundred men, you say? Well, we've quite a lot more mouths than that in this crowd. With the women and children there must be ten thousand. This calls for Moses and manna." Simon smiled good-humoredly. "Moses took care of a couple million people every day for forty years." He stood up to see if any of the people were leaving. They weren't, and sitting down again he offered another suggestion. "Perhaps we might have another catch of fish such as Simon Peter and the others had that day."

"There'd be no time to clean and cook 'em."

"Well, it's obvious Jesus isn't going to send these people away; if anything, more people are streaming toward him. You'd better come up with something."

They climbed out of the boat and waded ashore. Getting the other disciples together, they discussed the matter, then pushed their way through the crowd to where Jesus was sitting.

Jesus listened as Philip gave him the grim figures. "Eight months' wages would not buy enough bread for each one to have a bite!"

"How many loaves do you have?" Jesus asked. "Go and see."

Asking around, they found none; but Andrew had disappeared, and in a few minutes he came back with a boy. All eyes were upon Andrew, and he looked as if he felt foolish. "Here is a boy with five small barley loaves and two small fish, but how far will they go among so many?"

The boy held the lunch in the palms of his hands, five flat cakes made of barley, the poor man's fare, and two fish the size of herring.

Simon looked at Philip, and they looked the other way to hide their embarrassment.

"Have the people sit down," Jesus said, indicating that they should sit in groups.

The disciples looked at one another hesitantly. "You heard him," Andrew whispered, and Philip followed the others into a huddle. "He's going to feed them," Andrew said, "and he doesn't want them disorderly, snatching and grabbing for the food."

"You really think so?" Philip asked. "How?"

"I don't know how, Philip."

The disciples decided to have the people sit in semicircles in groups of fifty or one hundred, the men separate from the women and children as custom demanded.

Before they had the multitude seated the sun was flooding the western sky with streaks of red and gold. There were a hundred groups of fifty and many groups of one hundred. Only then did Jesus receive the loaves and fishes from the boy. The Lord raised his eyes to heaven, and after giving thanks he began to break the bread and fill a basket. Remarkably, the bread did not fail as he continued to break it and place it in the basket. When that basket was full he motioned to Philip, who quickly borrowed another from a woman in the crowd. Holding it for Jesus, Philip watched in amazement as he filled that one, too!

Quickly passing through one group after another with the bread, Philip was followed by another disciple serving fish, for Jesus was multiplying the fish as well. As the multitude became aware of what was taking place, they were very quiet. Reverently, they reached for the food and ate it with care as if it were, indeed, manna from heaven.

The sky was darkening, the eastern sky tinged with an after glow before everyone was fed. Munching on fish and bread, Philip reproached himself for not realizing Jesus' power to provide a table in the wilderness as easily as a Moses or an Elisha.

When he was fully satisfied and could not eat another bite, Philip tossed a bit of bread on the grass. Then he stood up and, drawing in his breath, patted his stomach, gratified. Simon grinned at him. "I tell you, Philip, you should be a political activist like me—together we'd make Jesus king instead of Herod."

"So we could have free meals?"

"Sh-h-h, he's saying something."

Jesus' voice carried well in the hollow of the hills. "Gather the pieces that are left over. Let nothing be wasted."

Surprised at the order, Philip and Simon nevertheless took their baskets and began picking up bits and pieces of bread. "There's plenty more where this came from," Simon remarked, "I wonder why we have to gather the leftovers?"

"So as not to waste food. I remember when he made the water into wine, it was one cup at a time, not a cupful more than was drunk. He doesn't waste food or drink."

"What'll we do with these scraps?"

"Feed animals, I guess."

When the baskets were full, they carried them to the ship and Philip counted twelve of them. "Look at that, Simon. We've more fragments than we had food to begin with!"

The crowd on shore was suddenly astir.

Simon looked up. "What's happening?"

Above the commotion they heard someone yell, "Surely this is the Prophet who is to come into the world!"

Curious, Philip and Simon jumped overboard and rushed back onto the beach. "Something's going on," Judas told them. "Listen . . . they want to make Jesus king!"

"A great idea!" Simon exclaimed.

"Not so fast," Philip cautioned.

"Not so fast? Isn't this what we've been waiting for?" Judas asked.

Right away, Jesus commanded the disciples to get back in the boat and go ahead of him to Bethsaida while he dismissed the crowd.

Reluctantly, they obeyed. As they pulled away from shore they could see that the people were gathering up their things and leaving. Jesus was nowhere to be seen. "Isn't he coming with us?" Philip asked.

"He's not coming," Judas answered, a bitter rasp in his voice. "Don't you see him now? He's going up on the mountain to pray."

12

Walking on Water

TRULY YOU ARE THE SON OF GOD.

Scripture Reference: Matthew 14:22–32; Mark 6:45–52; John 6:15–21.

J udas was disgruntled and reclined on the deck, unwilling
to assist the others in getting the boat underway. Jesus had
missed his golden opportunity. He had fed the multitude in a
miraculous way, and the people were ready to take him by
force and make him king; but he refused. It didn't make sense,
and Judas knew Simon the Zealot and other disciples felt the
way he did, for they were reluctant to get in the boat—anxious
that Jesus take hold of the opportunity at hand. Jesus insisted
that they leave, saying he was going up in the mountains to
pray and would meet them later. When the others caved in
Judas knew there was no use holding out any longer.

The sun had sunk behind the horizon and all the color in
the sky had faded into the dusk of evening. In his soul Judas
felt the nighttime of depression settling over him, and he
was angry. One lone star shone in the twilight sky, and on
the far side of the lake there were reflections of twinkling,
tremulous lights along the shore. But nothing shone in the
darkness of his despair. Swift birds swooped past making
their last flights of the day, and Judas, so angry he could
swear, wished he could take one long flight and find himself
a world away.

So here he was, headed for Bethsaida to pick up Jesus, who
would meet them once he was done praying, then on to Capernaum. *What will come of it?* he asked himself. *Only another*

dreary round of preachments, the press of crowds, and the threat of persecution.

The boat was hugging the shore, one lone torch blazing in the dark. Judas turned his back to the others and lay on his side, watching the reflected blaze dancing on the water below.

A strong wind began blowing and the flame, battered by the wind, succumbed. *That's all we need,* Judas complained to himself, *a storm to keep us working half the night.* The ruffled waters began pitching, and Judas got up knowing the crew would need all hands. Landlubber that he was, he nevertheless knew about these sudden windstorms swinging down the valleys, rushing onto the water with such force boats capsized with the first blast.

He could hear the wind howling as it tunneled down the valleys hitting the lake, scooping up waves and thrashing them about. Already waves were peaking above the boatsides. *It'll be a big storm,* he thought, as he helped John and Simon haul down the sail. "No need to have it torn to shreds," John said.

Manning the oars, the disciples began the fight to keep on course, the wind coming at them from northeast and east, churning the sea in convulsive upheavals. Spray splashed over the ship's railing, drenching them to the skin; and Judas, gritting his teeth, strained against the oar. Up and over, pull, pull, pull; up and over, pull, pull, pull. In the darkness they lost sight of any other ship; Judas felt alone and helpless against the rushing wind.

Waves washed overboard, first one side, then the other; the boat bobbed like a cork, swept up and down, sideways and across. Frantically the men shouted back and forth. "There's no controlling it!" Simon yelled, panic-stricken.

As the wind increased, shrieking as it came, even the experienced seamen—James, John, Simon Peter, and Andrew—were terrified. With every plunge into the valley of a wave the little craft shuddered, trying to right itself. With the constant rowing, his back shot through with pain, the muscles in his arms twisted with cramps, Judas could not let up even though he was sure in his heart they would not survive.

For hours they struggled against the storm, bailing out the water that threatened to swamp the craft, hanging on for dear life as the boat was dashed about. Blown far off course and making no headway, hopelessly lost, they were at the mercy of the merciless sea.

Thaddeus, his face drawn white, shouted in Judas's ear, "Are we going to make it?"

Judas yelled back, "I don't know!"

Thaddeus turned to the fishermen pleading for an answer, but they offered no hope.

The disciples had been on the sea nine or more hours when the fourth watch of the night began, and there were yet a few hours until daybreak. The sea raged violently, and the exhausted men were at their wits' end. "We can't last much longer," someone said, and Judas thought, *We're surely going down*, and he steeled himself.

Suddenly there was commotion all around him, everyone screaming, "It's a ghost!" Wheeling around, he cried out in horror! Something in the shape of a human form was moving out on the water!

As they were crying out in fear, the visible spirit looked as if he would pass them by. Then a voice called out to them, "It is I; don't be afraid."

The voice sounded like Jesus! Judas strained to make sure, but in the darkness he could not, and a mountainous wave came between.

Peter, shaking from head to toe, shouted back, "Lord, if it is you, tell me to come to you on the water."

Above the roar and thrashing of the storm, they heard the command, "Come."

The disciples crowded along the boatside as Simon Peter hoisted himself up and dropped overboard. He landed on the water as if it were as solid as the earth! Judas couldn't believe what his eyes were seeing! Amazed, they watched as Peter took a step, then another, unmindful of the angry wind and water. But then Peter glanced about him and frightened by the heavy waves rushing toward him, began sinking! "Lord, save me!" Andrew leaned far over the side, reaching to help his brother.

Jesus came quickly to the rescue, reached out his hand, and lifted Peter up on his feet.

Judas smirked. *How like Peter to think he could walk on water!*

But Jesus did not scold Peter for getting out of the boat. "You of little faith," he said, "why did you doubt?"

As the two climbed into the boat, the wind died down. Peter averted his eyes from the crew and tried to dry himself with a towel that was as wet as he. The sudden halt to the wind and waves astonished the men, and they marvelled as the sea rocked to a standstill.

Judas manned the oar again the sea as gentle as a lamb. *Now we can hoist the sail,* he thought, and rested on the oar. The men around him were overcome with awe, worshiping Jesus and saying, "Truly you are the Son of God."

At least we're safe, he thought, and mouthed the words the others were saying.

By the time the sun was rising the disciples had brought the boat to land and were dropping anchor in Gennesaret. Just as Judas had predicted, when Jesus was recognized word spread, and in no time at all people were bringing their sick, begging to touch the edge of his cloak.

To think, he could be king, Judas thought disgustedly. And shaking his head he sauntered away from the crowd. He would go into town and find a place to sleep.

13

Malchus

AND HE TOUCHED THE MAN'S EAR AND HEALED HIM.

Scripture Reference: John 13; 18:1–13; Matthew 26:26–56;

Mark 14:22–50; Luke 22:17–54

T he juicy lamb tasted good after the unseasoned vegetables and unleavened bread, not to mention the wine, but Simon Peter could not enjoy it because of the troubling things Jesus was doing and saying. The first thing that disturbed him was Jesus going around the room washing the disciples' feet; and when Peter refused to let him, Jesus said he must or have no part of him. That ended the matter; Peter reluctantly let him have his way.

But that was not all. All through the evening Jesus repeatedly warned them that he would be betrayed and arrested. And he said he would die. In the face of all that Jesus tried to comfort them and promised them a divine Comforter, but it was all so confusing Peter felt anxious and troubled.

Then there was the argument among the disciples as to which of them would be the greatest. *Perhaps if they had not been arguing,* Peter thought, *Jesus would not have talked the way he did.* He told them, "This very night you will all fall away on account of me, for it is written: 'I will strike the shepherd, and the sheep of the flock will be scattered.' But after I have risen, I will go ahead of you into Galilee."

Peter was quick to assure the Lord, "Even if all fall away on account of you, I never will."

"Simon, Simon," Jesus said, "Satan has asked to sift you as wheat. But I have prayed for you, Simon, that your faith may not fail. And when you have turned back, strengthen your brothers."

Peter, shaking his head vigorously, protested, "Even if I have to die with you, I will never disown you." And all the other disciples said the same.

But Jesus did not agree. "I tell you, Peter, before the rooster crows today, you will deny three times that you know me."

Simon Peter was crushed, and Jesus changed the subject. Addressing them all, he asked, "When I sent you without purse, bag, or sandals, did you lack anything?"

"Nothing," they answered.

"But now if you have a purse, take it, and also a bag; and if you don't have a sword, sell your cloak and buy one."

"*Sell a cloak and buy a sword!*" Peter repeated, alarmed.

Jesus explained, "It is written: 'And he was numbered with the transgressors,' and I tell you that this must be fulfilled in me. Yes, what is written about me is reaching its fulfillment."

Peter didn't pretend to understand but, sensing danger, he reached beneath his girdle for the leather sheath strapped to his side and pulled out his sword. Holding it up for all to see, another disciple on the other side of the table, showed his.

"See, Lord," the other man said, "here are two swords."

"That is enough," he replied.

Carefully, because it was razor sharp, Simon Peter slipped the sword back in its case.

They were singing the Hallel, the last refrain of the Psalm, when Peter missed Judas Iscariot's rich tenor voice. He looked around the table, then remembered Judas had gone out to buy more food or to give something to the poor.

When the hymn was finished Jesus got up from the table, and Peter scrambled to his feet. He was first in line behind the Lord as they went out the door and filed down the narrow steps to the street below. In his heart Peter resolved that he would defend Jesus, whatever the cost.

They were turning the corner when John Mark came running after them.

"I heard you coming down the steps," he explained to Peter, "so I threw this sheet around me and came on as I was. Where're you going?"

Peter hardly glanced at the youth, annoyed that he wanted to tag along. "To the Mount of Olives."

"Bethany?"

"Who knows?"

They passed through the Upper City, taking long strides at a steady pace. Peter knew the route well; in fact, they had come that way earlier in the day when they came into Jerusalem from Bethany. As they passed through the gate the paschal moon rode majestically over the Mount of Olives, and stars studded the dark heavens. Smoke was in the air. Along the slopes of the Kidron Valley vine-dressers were burning limbs they had pruned from the vines, and blazing fires dotted the hillside. Jesus' words were ringing in his ears: "He cuts off every branch in me that bears no fruit, while every branch that does bear fruit he trims clean so that it will be even more fruitful."

When they did not cross the Kidron at the lower ford, Peter knew they were headed for the Garden of Gethsemane where Jesus often took them. As the Lord led them past one terrace after another, through the old gnarled trees, Simon Peter reached up and picked a branch from a limb. The willow-like leaves with their pale olive undersides made him think of Noah's dove and the olive branch in its beak. Its promise of peace seemed long ago and far away.

Gethsemane was a garden in the orchard of olive trees, an enclosure guarding an olive press, a stone vat. Peter once watched men processing olive oil there. A large upright stone with a hole in its center held a beam in place, which turned to press oil from the olives. Weights hanging on the beam determined the amount of pressure brought to bear, and the beam was pushed around and around to produce the stream of oil pouring into a basin.

When the little party reached the olive press Jesus stopped, and speaking to his followers, said, "Sit here while I go over there and pray." Then he beckoned Peter, James, and John to come with him, and walked away from the others.

When they were out of earshot the Lord paused, and in the pale moonlight Peter saw the look of anguish in his face; it stabbed him through with sorrow. As Jesus spoke he appeared to be on the verge of collapse. "My soul is overwhelmed with sorrow to the point of death. Stay here and keep watch. Pray that you will not fall into temptation."

As Peter watched the Lord making his way toward an outcropping of stone, so weak he nearly stumbled, his heart hurt as if it were being pressed in a vise.

A swift breeze swept through the trees, stirring the leaves and making them rustle. Their heads together, James and John huddled next to Peter, watching. Reaching the outcropping, Jesus got down on his knees then lay face forward on the ground. Groaning in agony he cried, "*Abba*, Father, everything is possible for you. If you are willing, take this cup from me; yet not my will, but yours be done."

The ache in Peter's heart was so heavy he could not bear it, and he tried to shut out Jesus' groans, close his eyes to the agony of the Lord he loved. Depleted emotionally, weary with a weariness known only to those who suffer profound sorrow, Peter found it hard to pray.

John nudged Peter and told him to look. There beside Jesus was an angel, lifting his poor head, giving him strength. Simon Peter watched them until tears blurred his vision. Rolling over on his back, he squeezed his eyes shut and tried again to pray.

Close by the tree, James had fallen asleep with his arms folded on his knees, his head on his arms. From the heavy breathing of the slumbering man, Peter knew James was emotionally exhausted, sleeping for sorrow.

Peter's own eyes were heavy, and as he was trying to pray his mind wandered. Often nodding, waking with a start, he struggled valiantly, while John, on the other side of him, was gently snoring. Repeatedly Peter jerked awake, only to fall asleep again. Try as he would he could not keep his eyes open.

The next thing Peter knew, Jesus was calling him. "Simon, are you asleep?"

Peter sat bolt upright. There before him was Jesus, drenched with sweat—droplets like blood beading his brow, his hair wet against his forehead; perspiration dripping from his nose and beard; his sweat-stained clothing sticking to his body.

"Could you not keep watch one hour?" he asked. "Watch and pray so that you will not fall into temptation. The spirit is willing, but the body is weak."

Weak as Jesus was, with all the symptoms of prostration, Peter feared for his life. *Is he going to die here in the Garden?* he worried. As the Lord turned and went away from them, Simon Peter thought to go after him but felt helpless to do so.

In a little while he heard Jesus praying again. "My Father, if it is not possible for this cup to be taken away unless I drink it, may your will be done."

He mustn't die, Peter thought. *Surely, God won't allow him to die—His death would serve our enemies only too well.*

Peter was reminded of something Jesus had said earlier in the week: "Now my heart is troubled, . . . and what shall I say? 'Father, save me from this hour'? . . . No, it was for this very reason I came to this hour . . . Father, glorify your name!"

And God had answered from heaven, "I have glorified it, and will glorify it again."

Peter's troubled and tired mind could not think it through, and he did not want to believe what he thought it meant. Sleep was a blessed escape, and though he tried hard not to give into it again, he failed.

Peter did not stir until he felt John shaking his shoulder. Opening his tired eyes he saw Jesus standing over him. Embarrassed, Peter looked up at him helplessly, not knowing what to say. James and John kept their eyes on the ground, too ashamed to look up. Jesus turned and walked away again.

The heaviness of Simon Peter's heart weighed him down, and a sob that lingered in his throat was choking him. He tried taking great gulps of air and stretching his stiff limbs to get awake. In a little while a chill wind started blowing, and he wrapped his cloak about his shoulders, snuggling his face down in its folds. *Where was I?* he thought. *Oh, yes, praying . . . Let's see . . . I must pray not to get into temptation. Well . . .*

The rustling of the olive leaves made him cover his ears so he could not hear. In the snug warmth of his cloak his mind idled . . . random thoughts drifted sleepily.

The next thing he knew Jesus was speaking in a strong voice, "Are you sleeping and resting? Enough! The hour has come."

The hour, Peter repeated to himself, *what hour?*

"Look," Jesus was saying, "the Son of Man is betrayed into the hands of sinners. Rise! Let us go! Here comes my betrayer!"

The three of them struggled to their feet, alarmed by the urgency in Jesus' voice, amazed at his renewed energy. Through the trees Simon Peter could see the flares of torches. His heart raced, and his hand flew to the hilt of his sword. People were coming up the same path they had followed to the Garden.

The disciples they'd left at the olive press came running straight up the hill, leaping terraces, racing to warn them. John Mark, among them, was shivering from the cold, naked as he was beneath the sheet.

As the enemies filed past the olive press, Peter could see glints of light on shields and helmets. Their muffled voices were excited, cautious. Soon he saw those in the forefront of the mob, steadily approaching brandishing heavy clubs and swords, blazing torches lighting their way.

Jesus moved to meet them. When they saw him they stopped, and for a moment, face to face, an uneasy quiet prevailed.

"I see Malchus," John Mark whispered.

"Who's he?"

"Servant of Caiphas."

"The high priest?"

"The high priest."

Jesus called out to the leaders, "Who is it you want?"

Officials from the chief priest answered, "Jesus of Nazareth."

"I am he," Jesus answered in a strong voice.

The crowd looked frightened and scrambled to put distance between themselves and Jesus.

The blood pounding in his temples, Simon Peter nervously gripped the sword.

Again Jesus asked, "Who is it you want?"

The answer was long in coming. Finally, from the middle of the crowd, someone called out, "Jesus of Nazareth."

"I told you I am he."

It was then that Judas stepped out from among the ranks and approached Jesus. Seeing his friendly face, Peter was relieved.

"Greetings, Rabbi!" Judas said, and kissed Jesus. Peter thought it strange that he kissed the Lord because that was not their custom. Nor did Jesus respond as Peter expected.

"Judas," he said, "are you betraying the Son of Man with a kiss?"

Then it dawned on Peter—*Judas Iscariot . . . the betrayer! I can't believe it!*

Quickly three arresting officers stepped forward, one of them Malchus. Frantic, the disciples asked, "Lord, should we strike with our swords?"

But Peter didn't wait. With his sword he took a whack at Malchus to cut his throat. The sword missed its mark, but the man was wounded—a thin trace of blood ran down his neck. Peter had only sliced the man's right ear.

"No more of this!" Jesus exclaimed. "Put your sword away! All who draw the sword will die by the sword." Reaching out, he touched the ear of Malchus and healed him.

Only those in the immediate circle saw what Jesus did, and the healing did not interrupt his scolding. "Do you think I cannot call on my Father, and he will at once put at my disposal more than twelve legions of angels?"

Peter felt rebuked, but there was no time for self-pity—they were looping a rope around Jesus' wrists, tying his hands! The Lord looked at his disciples, his voice determined. "Shall I not drink the cup the Father has given me?"

Then he said to the officers, "If you are looking for me, then let these men go."

When someone grabbed John Mark, snatching away his sheet, Peter broke and ran. They were running and falling down the hill, leaping terraces, ducking limbs. John Mark passed Simon Peter, running naked through the Garden.

Finally, out of breath, and seeing that no one was chasing him, Simon Peter slowed down and tried to get his wits about him. *I'll keep a safe distance,* he decided, *and follow Jesus—see where they will take him.*

John

THROW YOUR NET ON THE RIGHT SIDE OF THE BOAT AND
YOU WILL FIND SOME.

Scripture Reference: John 21

J ohn, in the light of a torch, was intent upon seeing any sign of fish in the water below the boat, and held his spear at ready. Disappointed that they were not catching anything in the dragnet trailing behind the boat, several disciples had resorted to the spear but none of them had snared a fish.

John and some of Jesus' other followers had come to Galilee because Jesus had told them to and promised to meet them there. Waiting for him to come, Simon Peter announced that he was going fishing, and it seemed to James and John like a good idea to join him. Four other disciples climbed in the boat with them, and they set out about sundown.

But now the night was far spent, and one by one the men were coming to the conclusion that they were wasting their time. Before daybreak they all gave up and gathered in the bow of the boat where there was room for them to stretch out a bit. Thomas, like the others, wanted to talk. "I wish he'd come. Now that he's alive again, it's mysterious the way he comes and goes."

"He said he would meet us in Galilee and he will," John said.

"I wonder where he is?"

"He could be anywhere—Bethany or heaven," James said. "The way he comes and goes . . ."

A southerly breeze filled the sail, and the boat rocked along, the gentle waves slapping its bottom with the old familiar rhythm. John filled his lungs with the good air and noticed that daylight was reaching the tops of the mountains on the north side of the lake. Soon they would be able to see the snowcapped crest of Mount Hermon. A flock of swallows was passing overhead. *If birds are flying,* he thought, *dawn is not far behind.*

Thomas asked, "I wonder if anyone else has seen him?"

"Probably," they said.

"Who?"

"How should we know?" James answered crossly. "He's been seen by so many, it stands to reason there'll be others."

"Well, let's see—who has seen him?" John began. "Mary Magdalene was the first to see him, wasn't she?"

"Yes," his brother answered. "She was first, then Cleopas and his wife walked to Emmaus with him."

"I saw him," Peter reminded them. He was folding up his outer garment, making a pillow of it. "I saw him that first day. It was after John and I went to the tomb and found it wide open, him gone, the keepers gone—"

John's voice was husky. "I tell you, I'll never forget going to that tomb. Even now I can remember how the grave clothes felt in my hand, how the napkin that had covered his face was folded and lying by itself . . . Peter, I think the truth dawned on both of us at about the same time, don't you?"

"You mean about the grave clothes and all?"

"Yes. When we saw the winding sheet there we realized that grave robbers wouldn't have troubled themselves to un-wrap the body nor take such pains as to fold the napkin. I remember how Simon Peter and I looked at each other, afraid to say what we were thinking."

"I was overwhelmed; I couldn't say anything." Peter grinned. "Imagine me, Simon Peter, speechless!"

"I still didn't know what to believe, did you? Not until we were all in the upper room and Jesus came in without so much as opening the door did I begin to be convinced."

Nathanael smiled. "I thought he was a ghost until he

reached over and took that piece of fish and ate it. I couldn't believe my eyes when he started eating that fish—pulling out the bones and laying them beside his plate."

"I wasn't there," Thomas reminded them. "It was the next week before I saw him."

"You felt his wounds, Thomas. What was that like?" Nathanael asked.

Thomas closed his eyes, rubbed his head, trying to find the words. "Scars—you know, the nails made gashes. You saw them. I can't describe how I felt when I touched those wounds, all I could think about was, 'His flesh is as warm as mine—he's alive, he's alive again!' " Marveling still, he shook his head. "I wish he'd hurry up. Do you think he might be in Galilee now?"

"In Cana I heard Jesus visited his brother James," Nathanael said. "Have any of you talked with him?"

No one had.

"We ought to go see James."

Thomas drew a long breath. "Well, what do you think? Do you think he'll put Israel back in power?"

"He might," James said. "I wonder who'll be first in his kingdom?"

Simon Peter changed the subject. "I wonder if there'll be more miracles?"

"Why not?" James asked.

Peter shrugged his shoulders, folded his arms across his bare chest.

"I'm curious, too," Andrew said. "Miracles haven't always happened all the time everywhere. There has to be a purpose."

"I agree with you, Andrew," Nathanael said. "Before they crucified him, I think Jesus did miracles to prove he was the Messiah. Now that he's risen from the dead there'll be no further need for miracles."

Right away there were protests. "That's not true," James argued. "Jesus didn't do miracles only as signs. Don't you remember all those times when certain Jews wanted Jesus to

prove himself with a miracle and he wouldn't do it? And, most
of the time, when he did heal someone or raise them from the
dead, he told them not to tell anybody. How can you say, then,
that he did miracles to prove himself?"

"Well, who else ever opened the eyes of a man born blind,
or walked on the water?" Nathanael argued.

James was puzzled. "What're you getting at?"

"Just that. Miracles prove Jesus is who he says he is."

"Well, of course, but that's not to say he did miracles *only*
to prove who he is. There were other reasons as well," James
insisted. "As we all know, Jesus healed the sick and raised the
dead out of compassion, and I daresay he'll do it again."

"Perhaps," John said. "But he's already done so many miracles that if every one of them were written down, I suppose
that even the whole world would not have room for the books
that would be written."

James, like a dog with a bone, was intent on continuing his
side of the argument. "Besides, if Jesus did miracles only to
prove who he was, why did he feed all those people and then
walk away when they wanted to make him a king? Why didn't
he stand up then and there and declare himself the heir to
David's throne? I ask you now, answer me, Nathanael."

"I still say his miracles prove who he is: the Son of God."

James sighed. "We've been over that, Nathanael. Take the
case of Judas—he saw every miracle we saw, but did it make
him believe? No, indeed. He believed the miracles were real all
right, but he didn't care to submit himself to Jesus as Lord. I
contend that we believe the miracles because we believe Jesus
is the Christ and not the other way around."

Smoke from the burning pitch made John's eyes smart, and
he moved the torch out of his way. The argument had reached
an impasse, and he was glad because quarrels wearied him.

The little boat rocked on the water, the eastern sky now
light enough to show the outline of mountain against sky. The
morning star hung alone, its brilliance fading, and John was
looking forward to food and sleep.

He was thinking about breakfast when he heard someone on shore calling out to them, "Friends, haven't you any fish?"

They shouted back, "No."

"Throw your net on the right side of the boat and you will find some," the stranger told them.

The fishermen looked at each other dubiously. True, sometimes a person on shore could see a school of fish not visible from the boat, but in the predawn darkness that seemed unlikely. James complained, "That's all we need—some landlubber telling us how to fish." But he fell in with the other men, gathering up a net and carrying it across to the right side of the boat.

As they readied the net for casting, John held a torch over the side of the ship trying to see if there was some promise of fish but saw none. As the men unfurled the net and let it go, it spread out in a perfect arc, landing expertly in a full circle. Sinkers sank the net and on the surface of the water floats marked its course.

The fishermen decided it was time to draw in the net, and working in concert with the men at the other end John, at Peter's side, began pulling, tugging against the weight of a full catch of fish. While they were struggling to get the fish aboard, the thought flashed into John's mind that Jesus was the man on shore! "It is the Lord!" he exclaimed.

Peter dropped the net, ran across the deck, snatched up the garment he'd left there, wrapped it around his body, and dived in the sea.

"Where's he going?" Andrew yelled.

"That's Jesus. He's going to Jesus," John answered.

"Jesus? The Lord?"

"See for yourself."

In the early morning light they could see the man piling wood on a fire and there was no mistaking that it was Jesus. "It is the Lord!" they repeated.

"Don't you remember the last time we caught fish like this?" John asked.

"I do," said James, straining to lift the catch. Heaving together they poured pounds and pounds of fish into the boat. Standing knee deep in the heap of lively fish, James grinned. "The last time we had a catch like this was when Jesus borrowed Peter's boat—"

"Come on, let's get going," John said impatiently.

Setting the sail for shore, they were underway again. John watched Simon Peter as he was wading up on the beach. Jesus was walking toward him.

The ship glided closer to shore, the sun catching her sail, and John smelled bread baking and fish frying. As he watched the Lord and Simon Peter walked back to the fire. A lump rose in John's throat as he saw the Lord bending over the coals, preparing breakfast for them. *So like him,* he thought, and the joy of it brought tears to his eyes.

CHRISTIAN HERALD
People Making A Difference

Christian Herald is a family of dedicated, Christ-centered ministries that reaches out to deprived children in need, and to homeless men who are lost in alcoholism and drug addiction. Christian Herald also offers the finest in family and evangelical literature through its book clubs and publishes a popular, dynamic magazine for today's Christians.

Our Ministries

Family Bookshelf and **Christian Bookshelf** provide a wide selection of inspirational reading and Christian literature written by best-selling authors. All books are recommended by an Advisory Board of distinguished writers and editors.

Christian Herald magazine is contemporary, a dynamic publication that addresses the vital concerns of today's Christian. Each monthly issue contains a sharing of true personal stories written by people who have found in Christ the strength to make a difference in the world around them.

Christian Herald Children. The door of God's grace opens wide to give impoverished youngsters a breath of fresh air, away from the evils of the streets. Every summer, hundreds of youngsters are welcomed at the Christian Herald Mont Lawn Camp located in the Poconos at Bushkill, Pennsylvania. Year-round assistance is also provided, including teen programs, tutoring in reading and writing, family counseling, career guidance and college scholarship programs.

The Bowery Mission. Located in New York City, the Bowery Mission offers hope and Gospel strength to the downtrodden and homeless. Here, the men of Skid Row are fed, clothed, ministered to. Many voluntarily enter a 6-month discipleship program of spiritual guidance, nutrition therapy and Bible study.

Our Father's House. Located in rural Pennsylvania, Our Father's House is a discipleship and job training center. Alcoholics and drug addicts are given an opportunity to recover, away from the temptations of city streets.

Christian Herald ministries, founded in 1878, are supported by the voluntary contributions of individuals and by legacies and bequests. Contributions are tax deductible. Checks should be made out to Christian Herald Children, The Bowery Mission, or to Christian Herald Association.

Administrative Office: 40 Overlook Drive, Chappaqua, New York 10514
Telephone: (914) 769-9000

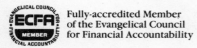 Fully-accredited Member
of the Evangelical Council
for Financial Accountability